D1277580

Journal of an Outlaw

Written by Mick McArt
Cover Art: Matt McEntire

MICK ART
PRODUCTIONS llc
PUBLISHING

Journal of an Outlaw
All Rights Reserved
Copyright © 2017 Mick McArt
V1.0

ISBN: 978-0-9915660-5-1
Library of Congress Control Number: 2017904547

Published by
Mick Art Productions, LLC
www.mickartproductions.com

PRINTED IN THE UNITED STATES OF AMERICA

FOR ALL THE DREAMERS,
ADVENTURERS, AND CREATIVES
IN THE WORLD WHO INSPIRE
AND INFLUENCE US ALL.

REVIEWS FROM THE REALMS

"I read it seven times!"
> – Drake Sharpenstick, The Hydra Perspective

"Not only did I find this to be an entertaining read,
I now use it to kill spiders!"
> – Miss Tuffet, Whey Farer Magazine

"The best read on the web..."
> – Terry Anchula, Arachnid Times

"I read it until I passed out!"
> – Stabbing victim from Derek the Cleric's waiting room

"I savored every word!"
> – M. Crawley, The Termite Prospectus

THANK YOU'S

God for my gift of creativity, my wife Erica McArt who brings consistancy and heart to the Unremembered Realms, my sons Micah & Jonah for their input (though they may not be aware of it), & my sweet daughter Emerald, Mike McEntire for the great cover art and Todd Lockwood for his advice and helpful tips about the art, Chuck Bailey, Mike Moore, Mark Johnson, Keith Mansfield, Roy Hoin, Brian Green, Kent Welhoff, Mike & Marilyn Johnston, Curt Coker, Howard Scholtz, Keithan Jackson, Jenny Bruzewski, Don Pentz, Tony Serra, Shirley Moore, Jerry & Sally Mansfield, Mike Gay, Patrick Brown (for playing Dwarf Mountain with me when I was a little kid), Vern Dalecki, Mitch Brown, Brian Lenz & The Boardgame Group, Shai Victor, Tony Harvey, Jason Anderson, Andrew Falconer, Dan from Radio Free Borderlands, Dungeons & Dragons Fifth Edition Facebook Group, Tabletop Role-Playing Group on Facebook, TSR/Wizards of the Coast for influences, and last but not least Jennifer Bouchard who proofs and tries to make sense of all this!

Mick Art Productions Publishing
www.mickartproductions.com

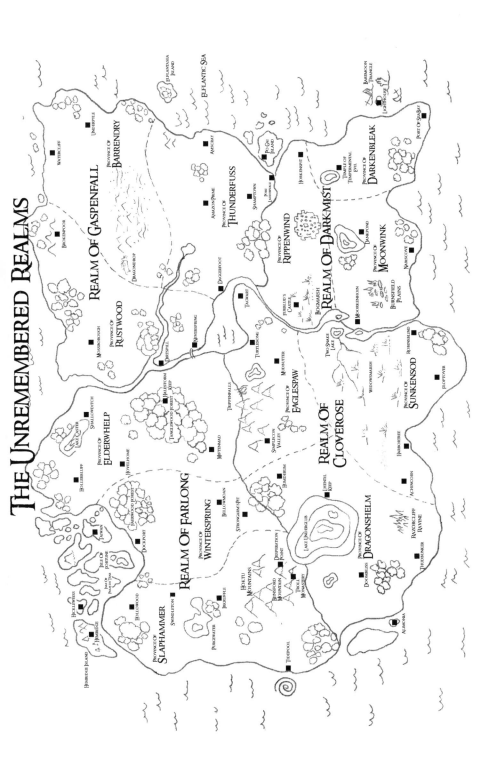

The Unremembered Realms

Realm of Gaspenfall
Province of Barrendry
Province of Rustwood

Realm of Thunderfuss
Province of Rippenwind

Realm of Darkmist
Province of Darkenbleak
Province of Moonwink

Realm of Cloverose
Province of Eaglespaw
Province of Sunkensod

Realm of Farlong
Province of Elderwhelp
Province of Winterspring
Province of Slaphammer

Realm of Dragonshelm

Waterliff
Underfyle
Brokenpoor
Mossborough
Direspill
Winterspring
Daggerroot
Dragondrop
Amscray
Amazon Prime
Shamptown
Port Laundervale
Horkenspit
Temple of Temperamental Evil
Barbmoon Triangle
Lighthouse
Port of Seabay
Rippenwind
Boogmarsh
Darepond
Marsicove
Two Snake Lake
Firblud's Castle
Moorbisfourn
Moorbisfourn
Burnsfield Plains
Rebinnerland
Floptover
Widowsmarsh
Harbortree
Acherncorn
Tagmart
Turtlestone
Mudrutter
Triplefalls
Simpleton Valley
Brameburn
Hemsil Keep
Lake Underglub
Razorcliff Ravine
Thudbunker
Hallestorm Forest Keep
Tanglewood Forest Keep
Mittenmad
Shalllewitch
Lake Caster
Hayvelhome
Hollercliff
Bellowmoan
Strongarmspit
Desperation Point
Hoktu Mountains
Bensford Mountain
Troll Monastery
Doombliss
Fairwood Forest
Dockport
Isle of Fortune
Jack of Polish Pile Tree
Hollowood
Hickleywiss
Hombridge
Hombridge Island
Purgewater
Jigglefile
Swindleton
Taiwan
Thidpool
Almonia

EPILOGUE

In my life, I've been described as many things: outlaw, thief, ghost, cretin...but I'll leave it up to whomever reads this to decide for themselves what I am. I've seen the world; good, bad, and ugly. So I've decided to keep a journal. It's a way of remembering the people, places, and the things I've seen and hopefully putting my memories into some perspective.

The Unremembered Realms is a remarkable place, and I have seen most of it. You may find this journal disturbing, and perhaps you should. My friend is the blade, my blood is the poison, my soul is like a ... awe, forget the sweet talk, just lock your doors and watch your back!

These entries are not in any particular order. I have only numbered them for your reference. When you've done as much as I have, it's easy to forget the details of when things have happened, only that they did. I did not change the names to protect the innocent, well, because no one is innocent.

Entry 1

...ig a rogue, you sometimes have to be clever and come up
...ways to make a few extra coins. One of my most reliable tricks
...head down to the local tavern. The bigger the crowd of pa-
...s the better. Bide your time until you overhear some locals dis-
...ing something that they think is important and then butt in.
...an take whatever side you want, but I always try to side with
...ggest guy in case things get real nasty.

...en someone else in the tavern makes an opposing viewpoint,
...pretend to take major offense to it. With a few mocking words
...the right tone, I can guarantee you're going to have a fight.
...dlocks are a thief's golden opportunity. While the aggressor
...ks he's got you, he's not paying attention to where your hands
...I've nabbed many a coin purse, whilst being choked. Being
...kled is even better! Also, don't be afraid to take a few punches
...re and there. It can be well worth it when the local rubes jump
...to back you up.

...Learn to roll with the punches, too. Take a hit, then roll around
...n the floor, while checking for gold teeth that have been knocked
...ut. Even on a bad night, you might get a few regular teeth, which
...s okay, because you can stick them under your pillow at night for
...few extra coins in the morning!

Entry 2

Dungeons seem to be a dime-a-dozen. Every evil wizard or captain of some horde is building one. The problem is that most of
these efficiency builds were rather small in size and didn't leave
much room for maneuvering. One time, this worked in my favor. I
was raiding Strongarm's Pit in the province of Farlong and trying
to get around a barbarian named Manhill the Large. He wasn't
known for being the brightest torch on the wall, but he was huge,
strong, and made a good shield.

His large frame was blocking up the hallway in front of me. I
could tell someone or something was in front of him firing arrows
and shooting spells. I could hear lots of shouting and screaming. I

1

jumped up and down trying to see over him, but all I could
were lights flashing and blood spurts splattering on my face.
could hear the horrid splats from Manhill's giant spike club a:
murdered whatever it was we were encountering.

After becoming frustrated, I became a little bored, so I sat do
behind him, kicked up my feet, and started working on the ma
for this journal. After a few minutes, I heard some fire spells e
ploding and noticed the big guy was starting to smell like me
butter and wet boots. Then, things got deathly quiet. Manhill
started yelling. Then, I heard a big thunk.

When I looked up at the back of his head, I saw an arrow tip
sticking out of it. Manhill fell forward and crashed to the groun
with a giant boom. I grabbed my rusty dagger and prepared for
worst, but there was no one left standing. Scattered around the
hallway were a dozen or so dead bodies. Half were smashed int
pulp, and the other half probably wished they would have been.

There were orc fighters, an ugly old bugbear, and a couple of
human spellcasters who had the stuffing knocked out of them.
"My back..." came a voice from somewhere near Manhill's body.
"My back is broken."

When I walked up to where I thought the voice was, I noticed
someone lying halfway underneath the large fighter's body. The
mysterious figure was nearly invisible because it was wearing a
magical blending cloak and holding a broken bow. "That's so
cool!" I told the dying rogue. "Mind if I try it on?"

I managed to get it off of him before he gasped and muttered
something indecipherable. Poor fool was a good shot, but obvious
not fast enough to get out of the way of my falling comrade. I
slipped myself into the dark cloak. It didn't have a scratch on it
and was a perfect fit. "My cloak," the dying man bellowed, "a thou-
sand curses be upon youuuu ... ugh," the rogue gasped before
dying, his eyes glazing over in their final angry stare at me.

I have to admit it bothered me a little, this low-level robber having such a cool item. I didn't even bother with the rest of the raid!
I quickly grabbed some coins from the other bodies, then used the
magic cloak to make a hasty exit. I did manage to use my new item
to scare a few remaining orcs so bad that they wet themselves.

Entry 3

ised to travel quite a bit with an older halfling named Chip. He
.s a happy little guy and fast on his feet. He would run with me
ter treasure until he was completely exhausted. It was many a
ight when I'd come into a tavern with a sleeping Chip on my
.houlder. The partnership didn't last too long, though, not many
of them do with me.

I was sold a map to an abandoned dungeon west of the edge of
he Barrendry Desert, by Chip's nephew, Robbie, the Thief. I
hought it sounded worthy of a look, so Chip and I agreed to go
check it out. Along the way, Chip told me of his upcoming retirement. "After the next big haul," he would say. I always laughed at
that because I knew he wasn't talking about gold, but of landing a
big halfing gal with whom he could settle down.

We weren't far into the dungeon when Chip waved for me to
slow down a minute while he ran ahead to check something out. It
wasn't well lit, and I had learned to trust the halflings' ability to see
in the dark. I waited for a few minutes but heard nothing. "Chip!" I
whispered loudly, but no answer.

I decided to move ahead and see what he was doing. I reluctantly
lit a torch and found that I had almost walked into a giant man-
eating jelly cube, a rare dungeon danger. I had only heard rumors
of these monsters, but here was one right now, only a few inches
away from me. When I backed off, I could see Chip had walked
head first into the thing. I tugged at him by the boots trying to get
him out, but it was no use. The mysterious creature wouldn't let go,
and I ended up on my backside holding a pair of boots with lightning bolts embossed on the sides. I had heard these jelly-like
cubes were slow, but I wasn't about to stick around and find out.

I let Robbie know about his uncle, and he was mad at first. Then
he asked me about Chip's special boots, but I just played dumb. I
kind of figured these boots to be magical, so I decided to keep
them for myself. No halfling runs that fast without a little help. It's
a good thing halflings have such big feet because these fit me well.

3

Entry 4

In my earlier days, I was hired by this dwarven cleric, named Dimwood to help him and a barbarian named Argenfall to go on rescue mission into the swampy region of Sunkensod. Apparently some lizard men had captured some halflings, and it was up to us to make sure they got back to their home near Lake Underglub alive.

Not long into our journey the pranks started. I'm not one for pranks; they never turn out the way I expect, but Dimwood was obsessed. He kind of feared Argenfall's hammer, so he saw me as a safe target. I thought clerics were supposed to be wise? He would tie my bootlaces together, dip my hand in warm water while I slept, and hide worms in my sandwiches. Argenfall would laugh for hours at these pranks, while I just steamed, plotting surprises of my own. Then, one night, while they slept, I switched the bottles on Dimwood's Potion of Ogre Strength and his insto-flow magic constipation medicine. I thought that would be good for a laugh.

By the morning, I had forgotten about my little trick, because we woke up to nearby screams. We hurried through the dirty swamp waters and spied four lizard men who had a small wagon with a cage filled with our missing halflings. They outnumbered us, but we were feeling confident that we could pull off a rescue.

They proposed that I sneak in using my shadow skills, while they created a diversion. They wouldn't tell me their plan, so I snuck around through the marsh and waited. Once they heard my bird-call signal, the barbarian stood up, waved his hammer, and shouted some taunts at the lizardmen who immediately started to race in their direction.

I have to admit, Argenfall was looking brave and ready to fight when Dimwood handed him the potion of Ogre Strength. That's when I remembered my prank. Oops. I heard a whole lot of yelling and other noises, but I ignored them and took off with the halflings in the wagon. I got them back to their hometown where I collected a sizable reward. I don't know what happened Dimwood or Argenfall, but I wasn't about to stick around for that mess.

∗ ∗ ∗

Entry 5

Tavern latrines are not known for their cleanliness, let me tell you! Most of the time, they are an adventure unto themselves. I was beginning to regret not staying at the Maplecliff just down the road. The Slimebarrell Tavern just screamed of unpleasantness, but the room was cheap...and so was the food, apparently. So there I was, after my second helping of Eggwin's Mystery Plate, and oh man, did I have to go.

So did the vastly overweight half-orc sitting next to me. He must have eaten the same thing because he did not even acknowledge my presence. He would grunt, groan, and clench the bench before letting out a foul stench that would turn the dead! Maybe he was some kind of bathroom cleric. You never know in the Unremembered Realms; I've seen much worse. I'd plug my nose and hold my breath as much as I could, but this two-holer outhouse should have been marked condemned a long time ago!

I plugged my nose and made some gagging noises as I left. The half-orc just gave me a dirty look and kept groaning. I made it out the door before I passed out and vowed never to go back. I was heading back into the tavern to strangle the cook, but then I spotted a new food shop down the road called "Thorax's Discount Meats." I paused, and then changed direction, "Today is Eggwin's lucky day," I grumbled to myself.

A few moments later, I was in the shop browsing his fine selection and nibbling on some samples. Thorax stood there watching me with a huge grin, piercing me with his eyes. He was a large man of almost seven feet tall. His huge muscles were covered with sweat, and even a bit of blood that must have spilled during the butchering process. "Are these fresh?" I asked.

"Screaming fresh!" he replied, his smile growing wider, like he was remembering something wonderful.

"I'll take a Journeyman's Feast, please, but be sure to use the freshest cuts." I demanded.

Just then, the obese half orc wandered past outside the window and stuck his tongue out at me. I think Thorax thought it was meant for him though. The shop owner's grin quickly changed to a frown. "Sure thing," he said, quickly moving towards the door. "Come back in the morning and I'll have some jerk, I mean, jerked for you."

I returned the next morning to find that he had all the meats packaged for me which fit neatly into my pack. I ate well for a week, thanks to Thorax. The meat had a slight odor to it, but I'm not one to complain; anything was better than eating at Eggwins again. My stay at the Slimebarrell Tavern improved as well, my latrine associate was gone. The half-orc must have joined a party and left. Even though he was gone, I somehow still felt a connection, like a piece of him was still with me.

Entry 6

Staring. It can make people mad, curious, or just uncomfortable. Especially the ladies. I love it when some snooty elf gal comes over and slaps my face. They don't even pay attention to the fact that I'm picking their pockets before they storm off in a huff. You've got to pick your target carefully though. This technique doesn't work so well on female ogres or medusas.

Entry 7

Being a rogue has its ups and downs. In one town, I'm a hero for helping a party on some dungeon raid, and in the next, there are "wanted" posters of me hanging all over the place. I remember meeting Palmaltheus, the Mayor of some stink town, and he proudly handed my group the Key to the City. While the blowhard paladin of the group, I think his name was Longwind, was droning on about justice, heroism, or whatever, I pinched a few little baubles from dignitaries who weren't paying attention.

Knowing someone would eventually notice, I slipped the smallest bauble into a robe pocket of Grumptumble the Druid. Later, after the ceremony, I tucked my treasures away in the knot of a tree out back. When the authorities came looking, they all pointed at me, but I told them to search all of us, to be fair. You should have seen the look on that old druid's face when they were hauling him off, flared undertrousers filling the whole way!

Entry 8

I bought a map to a small island named Palm de Tear. It was located a short distance off the northwest of Farlong. "It's a hidden paradise," Robbie the Thief bragged, "with a hidden treasure!"

I didn't trust the halfing much; who knows where he got this so-called map, but I needed a vacation, and the thought of a hidden treasure was too enticing. As I rowed my small boat to the island's shoreline, I started to wonder why he sold me the map in the first place. Why didn't he just get it himself? But as I drew closer, I could see why. There were corpses scattered around on the beach. It didn't take long before I noticed one of them was still clutching a copy of a treasure map, just like mine.

Sitting in the middle of the corpses was a hole with an opened treasure chest in it, empty of course. "Oh well," I thought to myself. "Might as well make the best of it."

I poked around the corpses – humans, orcs, elves, and a few I didn't recognize. Not even a gold tooth was to be found. The island was beautiful, though, so I stayed a couple of days to do some relaxing on the beach, swimming, and eating coconuts with some fish I caught. The coconut did do a number on my stomach, though, so I used the treasure chest as a latrine then reburied it.

When I got back to the mainland, I spotted Robbie the Thief surrounded by a very tough looking gang of fighters. "Where's the map, thief?" the gap-toothed leader spat at Robbie. "We have to catch up with our gang!"

The little halfling started babbling, but I stepped up and handed Robbie the map. "Excuse me, gentlemen," I said in a raised voice, "I cannot accept this as payment at my trading shop, halfling. I would like my gold back please."

Robbie looked at me with a frown. "Give him his gold," the leader snarled while grabbing the map. "We've got a treasure to collect."

The large man reached down and grabbed Robbie's gold pouch, then handed it to me. "Don't worry about this pittance, halfling," he told Robbie. "You'll receive your fair portion of what's in the chest. Now come with us!"

Two of the men ushered Robbie forward, and when he looked at me he stuck out his tongue. I just smiled and stuffed his coin pouch into one of my cloak pockets. For once, I hoped Robbie and his new friends enjoyed their reward.

Entry 9

I was tied up to a tree and left for dead. Three days I was there, awaiting my doom. I didn't dare cry out in the middle of the Faerwood Forest because, the place was the home to many magical creatures. Some good, some incredibly deadly. When I wasn't sleeping, plotting my revenge, or getting circled by vultures, I chatted with the little wood faeries who lived in the trees.

It was obvious they had no idea what shhh or shush meant because all they would do is talk, talk, and talk. You would think these three-inch tall pests would help a guy out. Instead, they took turns telling me of all their life stories. I didn't care what their cousin in Tanglewood was doing, but they would repeat the story if I offered any objection.

Then they would whip out the family drawings, "Here's Aunt Myrtle sleeping in a dragon's ear," one exclaimed. "Oh, here's one of Uncle Cletis bird bombing a caravan."

For three days I endured their nonsense until my sweat had finally loosened the ropes. Before I ran off, I did learn a few secrets, though. Did you know that the wood faeries have spells for almost everything? Scrying, transforming, healing, invisibility, untying; you name it. Well, guess what spell they don't have. Unsquish!

Entry 10

So, this one night I was hanging out at Ol' Shrively's tavern with my associate whom I affectionately call Two Chairs. He's an obese lycanthrope who would always complain about the small portions of food being served.

I wasn't in the mood to hear the werewolf's whining, because I was still upset at him for eating my favorite tailor, who was only half done making a tunic that I had ordered; made special with well-hidden pockets. My anger subsided when he began heckling the annoying bard who was on stage for amateur night. Every time the would-be songbird tried to sing and play his lute, Two Chairs would belch or break wind loudly.

The bard would frown and try to ignore us, but it was hard to avoid the gaze of the giant werewolf, who was licking his lips at him. "Hey, Screech! How about a bite after the show!" Two Chairs would shout.

The werewolf howled out with laughter so boisterously that he fell over and landed on top of me. I guess a riot broke out at that point and all I can remember is Two Chairs beating a constable over the head with the bard's arm, while it was still holding the lute!

I woke up the next day in a cell with Two Chairs in his human form. After paying the fine, he took me to his favorite tailor and hooked me up with a fancy tunic. "Wow!" I said, admiring the stitch work. "This guy is great!"

"I hope so," Two Chairs said while handing the tailor some coins. "I plan on eating him later!"

Entry 11

I remember one time when I came across a particular well in the heart of Lhentil Keep. My guild brother, Aggression, and I stood about twenty paces away from it watching hopeful people make wishes as they tossed coins into the water. It was such a beautiful thing! I have to admit that it almost brought a tear to our eyes to witness such a momentous occasion.

Can you imagine? Not only could we steal their coins, but probably their wishes as well! Aggression was not convinced that this was for real, so I challenged him to toss in a copper, I mean, we'd just steal it back later, come sundown.

So, he casually walked up to the well, turned slowly back to me with a suspiciously menacing grin, and tossed the coin. He just stared at me for a minute, with those steely grey eyes, then began to frown.

"Did it work?" I asked.

"We'll see," he replied with a half-smile.

Later that night, after a quiet dinner at a sleepy little tavern nearby, we made our way back to the well.

The sun had set, and it was dark when we both waded knee deep in and started filling our sacks. I wondered if the wish thing was real. "Psst...Hey, Aggression. Find any good wishes?" I chuckled.

That's when I noticed he wasn't there. But, in his place, were a few angry constables with their swords drawn. I dropped my sack of coins back into the water and made a desperate wish of my own, before they carried me off by my elbows! As I was being led away, I looked back to see Aggression deftly picking up the sack and grinning at me. That's when I knew his wish came true. The dirty cheat.

Later on, my own wish came true when they threw him in that cold, dark cell with me. We both agreed that the well was a mighty power that should never again be tampered with.

Entry 12

The moonless night was perfect for my group to sneak in through the sewer system of a spooky castle in Moonwink. It was dank, dark, and reeked like everybody's business, but the rumors of great treasure helped us to endure the stench. The castle radiated not only with the pungent stink of raw sewage, but with an aura so evil that it could be felt down to your bones! I wasn't scared, though, Fizzledoubt the wizard was confident that we could gain access to the treasure room without facing any of the monstrosities of this place.

He had hired Dungbar the half-orc, a fellow rogue who guided us through a couple of long tunnels, before we ended up in a dark room with steps leading out of the waist deep sludge and up to a platform with a door. If you haven't figured it out yet, Dungbar was a traitor and leading us all into a trap.

Dungbar said there was a hallway beyond the door and that he would use his shadow skills to see if there were any guards. The paladin, wizard, archer, and cleric all agreed to wait as he slipped through the thick, wooden door. Then, I heard a click after he locked the door behind him. Dungbar watched through the small barred window of the door as a large group of sewage zombies rose up out of the water and slowly approached our party.

Dungbar laughed loudly and held up the magical access key in front of the window, as he shouted taunts at my doomed lot. Poor Dungbar. He didn't see me using my own shadow skills, as I followed him when he went through the door!

Moments later, he was on the other side, facing the zombies with an "Eat me" sign stuck by a small knife into his back. He got bit a few times before I watched him do a triple flip, diving back into the raw sewage to get away. I held my nose and gave his performance a thumbs down, but the sewer zombies must have been impressed, because it seemed they were hungry for more.

Entry 13

What I like about wizards is that they usually have a lot of expensive stuff I can hawk for a few coins at some local flip-n-wink for a few coins. The problem is getting it away from them! The easiest way, is to go with a group into a dungeon, pretending to care about their cause, then hide in the shadows during most of the combat. If I'm quick enough, I can pilfer what I can, while the head honcho is casting his nastiest conjurations at the rest of my party.

The trick is, not to stab him in the back before getting some good stuff. That's because the wizard who is with you will want to lay stake on all evil creep's items, claiming he's the only one able to use them, which is not true at all! As far as I'm concerned, any magic item I find can easily be traded for gold!

I remember this particular battle where I snuck up behind a wizard and switched out his Flaming Breath Potion with a small vial of a sample I was saving for my checkup at my local cleric's office. I guess you'd call it a potion of bad breath now. I don't think the evil wizard appreciated the gag, though! You should have seen the look on that wizard's face before Percival MacLeod, our party's paladin, smashed his groin in with a kick from his heavily armored war boot!

Our wizard was disappointed, though, wondering where all the evil one's magic items were. I just shrugged, trying not to let the wand that I just stole poke out of my cloak! He ended up muttering some curses and settling for the fallen spellcasters hat and socks.

Later, I felt sorry for him later when I heard that the socks turned out to be the cursed and unremovable Footbane Soaker Socks of Achincorn! Apparently, it's what had driven insane the evil wizard that we killed.

Entry 14

How do you go from a "Help Wanted" flyer to a "Wanted" one? Let me explain.

I was a bit down on my luck and looking over some village community board in Floptover, when I found a Help Wanted ad for a potion tester. It was down at Big Al's Discount Alchemist shop just around the corner. Usually, I wouldn't touch this with a 10-foot staff, but I was broke and in need of coin. The business hadn't made any progress creating useful magical potions, so they were desperate to have people to experiment on.

The payments were good and on-time, but the side effects left me a little bit nervous to continue. For one thing, I grew a sixth toe on my left foot, and one potion put me to sleep for a while...two months to be exact. When I finally woke up, I noticed my beard had grown long, and I was so hungry I could eat roadkill...again.

Big Al and his assistant alchemists had left me up on a table and were nowhere to be seen at the moment. I was thirsty and still kind of out of it when I started to drink out of all the vials I could find. I don't remember blacking out, but I remember waking up floating three feet off the floor with objects spinning wildly around me.

The owner came bursting through the door with his lackeys trailing behind him. They were shouting and clapping their hands in excitement. After the cheering, high-fives, and secret handshaking, they huddled together whispering. They all turned to face me, holding these long daggers. "Don't be afraid," Big Al said calmly, with a growing smile. "We only want to find out what you drank..."

Just as they closed in, I managed to use my mind to whip the flying objects into them, knocking them all unconscious. Using my new powers, I flew from the room with all their coins in tow; they did owe me two months back pay after all.

Even though the effects only lasted a couple more hours, I was happy to discover that something special happened. I gained a small form of permanent telekinesis. I could move any small object within five or six feet, a real boon for a pickpocket like me!

Entry 15

When I was a young man, I would fall for a girl, once in a while. There was once this human archer gal that I found to be especially fascinating. She had an inner strength. Her name was Charisma, and she was as beautiful as she was intelligent. I knew that because she wouldn't give me the time of day. Well, it was kind of hard to blame her, after I had stolen her pocket watch five or six times!

She was fast too, very dexterous, chasing me down through those dark alleys. I referred to this as our nightly constitutional. I steal, she chases. She beats me up, I swoon.

Charisma showed great wisdom finally dragging my unconscious body to the local constable. I was in smitten and thought I would never give up on her! Well, that is 'till some ogre, named Gort, broke her heart...literally...with a giant club.

Entry 16

So there I sat, amongst all the dead and dying. It was one of the most brutal dungeon battles my mostly dead party had ever seen. Orcs, skeletons, kobolds, ogres, and even a couple dozen battered field mice lay bleeding over the floor of the orc king's treasure room. Only Fogbrain, that very king, and a few of his troops remained standing.

"Thank you for the battle, the treasure, and your heads!" he cried out in a nearly exhausted laugh. He was addressing me and my heavily wounded teammate, Bowhammer Strongwhiff. He noticed me crawling over to the dead cleric and ordered a warrior to stumble over and snatch the bag I was reaching for.

"Oh no, you don't," he said, before reaching into the bag.

"Potions of Healing...how wonderful!" he said, as he passed one around to each of his men.

They all gave each other a big toast for winning the battle and gulped down the magical brew.

"Now you dieeee....urggg," he choked before falling to his knees, his troops falling in unison.

Bowhammer looked at me in amazement. "Poison?" he stammered, breathing heavily. "How?"

"The cleric and I switched vials before the battle," I panted, pulling us out a couple of them from my pack. "Orcs aren't the cleverest race."

The orc's bodies all fell over with a thud at the same time, as we both clinked our vials together, before gulping down our potions.

Entry 17

I have a magic dagger I affectionately named Magurk. It's sharper than a dragon's tongue and just about as deadly too. I named it Magurk because that's the sound my enemies make as it finds its way into their back. I got it by rescuing the dreaded Two-headed Giant of Mossborough.

I had heard rumors of a magical dagger he had in his cave so I tracked him down and waited until nightfall. I heard snoring coming from the dark entrance, so I strolled in, feeling pretty confident. How was I to know that one head was narcoleptic and one was an insomniac? He, or they, began chasing me in the dark through the denseness of Tanglewood Forest and I ended up tripping over a log.

He stopped just in front of me and picked up the mentioned log to smash me, but it turned out the log was attached to a thick spider web. Two giant spiders immediately landed on him and started to bite. He managed to squash one before he was overcome by the paralyzing poison. I ran off as the spider began to cocoon him and headed back towards his cave.

There wasn't much at all, a dead cat, and three snot covered blankets he/they were using as handkerchiefs. I almost left, but I saw the shape of a dagger in one of the snot blankets. As I began to leave, I felt a little bad for the giant, so I grabbed some of his gear and headed back for the doomed creature. I didn't really like giants, but I despised creepy spiders.

When I got back, I could see the spider crawling over the top of the cocooned giant so I snuck up wearing my special blending cloak and threw a mucous-covered blanket on top the spider. As the spider struggled, I jumped up and plunged my new dagger deep into its back. "Magurk!" was the only sound it made before crumpling to the ground, eight legs twitching.

I cut the giant loose with the dagger, and he stood up quickly and grabbed me by the neck and held me up in the air. His mean grimaces turned soft when I held the dead cat up for them. They set me down, took the dead cat, and ran off back to their cave. I was happy about the dagger...and also about living, but I have to admit, I was already starting to miss that cat.

Entry 18

I could never stand tax collectors. Whoever the local king was, he made sure to find the biggest and deadliest killers to collect for him. Most of the time, I'd just hide, "Your fair share," usually meant a beating and quick trip to the poor house. It's even worse when it's not gold they want, but blood. You see, in Bogmarsh, the tax collector is a vampire, named Thurston Furblud.

He has many drones who go out during the day, and an army of ghouls who go out at night. They scour every village and hamlet taking blood donations for the lazy vamp. When I travel through the area, I always carry a pint of plague blood on me. A little white bogroot powder gives me that freshly drained look. If Thurston ever finds out that I'm the reason he spends half the night on a chamber pot...well, let's just say I hope he doesn't.

Entry 19

One time I was hiding out in a stable after visiting a local Druid jamboree. That's when the stablemaster, a smelly human named Bugbeard, told me of a secret monastery on one of the Hoktu Mountains nearby. He said it was rumored to have some great treasure, so I figured a journey like this could get me out of the area for a bit until things calmed down.

When I headed out, I rented a pack mule from Bugbeard. His odor could drop a hill giant at fifty paces, but he knew maps and was honest and gave good advice. He told me what he had heard about the treasure then started to warn me of some unusual trolls that had been encountered by other adventurers. I flipped him a Druid's copper, thanked him quickly, and took off before he could finish whatever boring tale he was most likely going to drivel on about.

It was a half-day's trek up the mountain, for most of which was clear with a slight nip in the air. It wasn't long before I lit a torch, just for a little extra warmth. As I came upon an open rest area, I encountered my first troll. It came out of the woods wearing a gray robe and wiggling its long, green finger at me, "Food! Come!" it cried loudly.

I didn't like the sound of that, so I broke a vial of oil and tossed it on it. The creatures eyes lit up when he felt the flame of my torch. As most of you know, fire is the only thing that can kill these horrid creatures. If you stab them, they'll just regenerate, then kill and eat you. As I watched it burn, it struck me as odd that it was wearing a robe. Trolls don't usually wear clothing; they were often covered in scabs, moss, or even mucous.

I poked around for any little treasures, but this one didn't have any. Must have killed a monk at the monastery and took his robe, I thought. Something told me today was going to be a strange one, indeed. Which, turned out to be true, because I ended up killing three more of the ugly beasts, before I finally made it to the monastery.

When I entered the temple, I was amazed by its vast and beautiful architecture. I was kind of giddy about the treasure, so I was caught off guard by the large, mysterious monk who approached me. He did a slight bow, which I hesitantly returned.

"What can I do for you?" he said in a raspy, harsh voice.

"I hear you guard some treasure," I answered.

I was kind of shocked when he pulled back his cowl and revealed that he too, was a troll. "I never heard of a troll monk," I said, scoping around for any sign of a treasure vault.

"We are indeed rare," he explained. "The trolls here at the temple have overcome our aggressive instincts. We've been training for decades to bring coexistence to the world."

"You don't' say," I said, suddenly realizing what I had done.

"The true treasure is inner peace," he spoke softly. "And I offer it freely to you."

"Inner peace," I repeated. "That don't sound lucrative, but I'll take what you got."

"We also have a rare magical armor...and few gems," he said, pointing to an intricately carved stone door. "These might be helpful for your journeys."

He could tell by my grin that I was impressed. "We'll have to wait,

17

though," he stated. "That stone door is magically locked; it can only be opened by the five troll monks who live here. A powerful wizard set this up for us."

"Five troll monks," I repeated his words, while getting a sinking feeling in my gut. "Where are the other four?"

"Oh, they go up and down the mountainside, enjoying nature and inviting new faces for food," he calmly replied. "There are so many hungry travelers out here; it's our way of being friendly. The others should be here soon, if you don't mind waiting."

As I excused myself, I turned around and started to walk away. That's when I noticed the half-burned troll walking into the temple. I quickly picked up my pace and made it out the door just in time to hear the head monk start to scream. "Kill every human!"

I quickly jumped on the mule and rode it down the mountain as fast as I could get it to move. It ran me all the way back down the mountain and returned us both to Bugbeard's stable. I was just about to walk in the door when vines exploded up from the ground and held me in place. Moments later I was surrounded by angry druids.

"This is him, Greentongue," one stated while pointing at me. "He's the one who picked our pockets."

"Where's our money, thief!" one of them shouted.

"Yeah, man," another stepped forward, "Give us back our coppers!"

I couldn't reach my dagger, so it looked like I would have to talk my way out of this one. "I donated them to the temple on the mountain," I said. "But if you want them back, just ask the peaceful troll monk about it, I'm sure he'd understand."

They seemed to calm down, as soon as I mentioned the monk. "That's cool," Greentongue said, and he released his vine spell. "I always wanted to meet the peaceful monk; he's a legend in these parts."

"Should we grab our weapons?" one of the druids asked.

"No need," Greentongue replied. "The five troll monks are very kind. I'm sure we'll be taken care of the minute we set foot inside the temple!"

Entry 20

Just for kicks, I decided to go into a new town dressed as a wizard. Even weaker spellcasters always seemed to get loads of respect in the Unremembered Realms. As a rogue, I'm lucky that people don't spit on me half the time! It just so happened that, while traveling a few hours earlier, I came across Fishcomb Coppertooth. He was an evil wizard in charge of Boglice the Orc, who had been raiding local villages. I thought I'd give his robes a whirl, since he'd no longer be needing them. I just hoped the people didn't notice the blood-stained hole in the back.

The tavern keeper greeted me with a smile and a thumbs up when I walked through the door. I liked this. He even offered me a free meal. After eating, I sat for a minute and contemplated my next endeavor. Who knows, I thought to myself, maybe I'll just leech off these rubes for awhile.

"Are you Fishcomb the Wizard?" came a stern voice as a man approached.

"Sure I am," I replied, as I turned around to see the town constable and his men approaching.

The tavern keeper was now frowning and pointing at me. "Oh boy," I thought to myself, this must be one of the villages he raided. They ended up taking me to their local jail, where I sat for the night, while they readied the gallows.

As I plotted my escape, Boglice's orc raiders showed up, killing everyone who got in their way. When they were fighting their way into the jail, I pulled the wizard's robe hood over my face. When they unlocked the cell door, I grabbed all my gear and followed them out.

On the way back to the orc camp, I ended up backstabbing them with my dagger, Magurk, and took whatever paltry coin these low-ranking soldiers had. I slew the last one just outside of their secret base. I was close enough to see Boglice, himself, pacing back and forth among a small group of his soldiers.

I took off the wizard disguise and headed back to the village, letting the constable know of Boglice's secret location. After his capture the city officials treated me to a warm meal and a show. The village people greeted me with cheers, as I took my place near the gallows. For once, I felt welcomed, and finally, respected! Even Boglice, the special guest, shouted at me, as they placed the noose around his muscular neck. I don't speak orcish very well, but I'm sure he understood how happy I was to see him "drop" by!

Entry 21

Hauling a load of treasure from the lowest part of a dungeon to an outside pack mule and wagon sure does a number on your back! I was almost relieved when the dungeon's master surrounded my lot of mostly thieves and took all the treasure back!

They led us to a dark torture room to find out where we were from, why we were there, told us to get ready to die...yada, yada. The torture master, Lungbutter Spittleface as I called him, shouted on and on about making me talk then proceeded to stretch me out on the torture rack. Wouldn't you know that it popped my back into place? I yelled out in relief, but he thought that I was in pain. He removed me and said there'd be more tomorrow. I couldn't wait.

Later on, our lone fighter, Mangleneck Pulsadrum, got loose and killed all the guards. I reluctantly left, but I have to tell you, I could've used a few more days of that torture! I wonder if Lungbutter does house calls?

Entry 22

Have you ever met a lady who just put a spell on you? I have. She was a real charmer. I got hired by a couple of locals to dispose of a den of evil clerics who had been hanging around the small village of Dankpond and raiding them with the undead.

The villagers also hired a lovely elf gal, named Silvara. She was a silver-haired wood elf with a nice smile and an assortment of magic trinkets. Together, we tracked down the evil cleric's hideout, which ended up being at an old cemetery, deep in the woods, by Dankpond. It was easy to spot, because all the graves were open from when the undead had crawled out.

"What's the plan?" I asked.

She turned to me, with a smile, and mumbled something, as her eyes glowed. Somehow, I felt compelled to do whatever she wanted me to. "It sure would be nice if you stopped those mean old clerics for me..." she suggested.

At the time, it seemed like the only logical solution. So, I snuck inside, ready for a fight. An hour later, I reappeared, bruised, bloody, and beaten up, but the clerics had been dispatched. "Thank you," she smiled. "You are a true friend."

I was happy that she was happy, for some reason. I even told her about the amazing magic items in my backpack. "Can I have the treasure?" she winked.

"I'd be delighted...utterly charmed, to let you have them..." I said, giving her the loot.

To this day, I have no idea why I just handed it over.

Entry 23

Not many beings in my chosen profession live very long. As a matter of fact, finding someone close to my age is rare. Usually, somewhere along the line there is some critical fumble that takes them down, or they just don't possess the winning initiative to succeed. Mind you; it is not always their fault.

I remember coming fresh out of the Crimson Roof Thieves Guild with a couple of fellow graduates and being flat broke. When we did manage to swipe a few coppers, we'd head down to the local Copper Stop, which can be found in all the major cities of the Unremembered Realms. The equipment or weaponry you'd buy there was pretty flimsy, but if you needed something for a dungeon raid, it was the only place you could afford. Everything in the store was priced at only one copper coin! It was all manufactured by Bargon Gnomes on the Island of Taiwan, which is just off the northwest coast of Farlong.

I don't know how many young associates I'd lost because of the failure of these cheap items, but what choice does one have when starting out? I don't think I would have made it at all if a traveler I met hadn't recommended I go to the Starvation Army Surplus and pick up some gear there. To some, it was a desperate move, but they had good equipment if you could survive shopping there.

The trick to your local Starvation Army stores is surviving the visit in the first place. They have bell ringers out front, warning would-be customers to stay away. They'd always have a little red bucket, filled with a nice treat, usually nuts or berries, for the desperate shopper who might be willing to go in. "Almonds for the poor!" they'd shout out as they rang their bell.

They call it the Starvation Army, because it is run by a realm-wide network of the undead. The workers are usually zombies at some stage of decay and are still wearing various types of armor. Some still have weapons on them, like a sword still in its scabbard. The way to shop there is to run or sneak in, tackle one of the zombies, and take its stuff before the herd intercepts you.

Most would-be customers become "volunteers" there, if you know what I mean. During my first year out from the guild, I became a frequent shopper there. Almost all of my equipment and weapons came from some unlucky sap, who was no longer shopping, but stuck in layaway.

Entry 24

Have you ever been stuck waist deep in gold? You'd think it was great, except I was really stuck. What made the situation worse was that two heads of a seven-headed hydra were arguing over who got to eat me. One of the heads already swallowed my party's fighter, Dot Matrix, and was feeling full. Apparently, the other heads were on a diet or something, but these two were pretty adamant about who was going to crunch my bones for their snack.

Just as they came to an agreement to split me down the middle, something split the stomach of the hydra wide open...a Hydra-matic Blade of Sharpness. An ooze covered Dot pushed her way

22

out of the guts. She was smiling and holding a half digested orc arm. It had two magical looking rings. She tossed one ring to me and put the other one on herself. My advice to future hydras: if you're going to swallow someone whole, make sure they are not still holding their sword!

Entry 25

Have I mentioned that I wanted to kill Robbie the Thief? The toad-faced halfling sold me another fake map! This time, it was to a dungeon off the hillside of Brokenpoor. Apparently, some orcs had taken up residence there and were tormenting the locals. According to Robbie, the townsfolk were well-to-do, so this would be a good chance for some easy gold, plus justice for the orc's victims. The map and tip cost me some gold coins, but I thought the investment might pay off.

I snuck my way through a small tunnel that I found and hid in some shadows. I made my way down a long, maze-like tunnel before I encountered smooth brick. "Good thing I have this map," I thought to myself. I followed its confusing pattern and weird numbering system down two more levels before I realized that this wasn't a map at all, but a crossword puzzle that Robbie was too lazy to finish! I thought the letters inside the boxes were clues!

The returning horde came back before I had a chance to back out, so I had to use my Hat of Disguising to appear as a half-orc lice inspector. For two weeks, I spent most of the day picking lice off of orcs! Note to self: strangle Robbie while he's sleeping.

Entry 26

So, there I was, just to the north of Widowsmarsh, buried up to my neck in a shallow quicksand pit. I wish someone would have put up a sign; this stuff is dangerous...especially in swamp giant country! It was pretty thick, so I could barely move, but at least there was a solid bottom.

What was strange, was the foul odor, plus I kept bumping into random bones. That didn't make me feel any better. Whatever left these here, probably used this as a trap to snag food. After a while, a couple of gnolls, commonly known as half-dog men, noticed me and laughed. At least they didn't kill me. Then, a small group of Cagin' Dwarves came by and pointed at me, speaking in their undecipherable marshland drawl. They are called Cagin' Dwarves, because they enjoy capturing their enemies in cages.

I pleaded with them, "I really need to go!"

My predicament made them roar with laughter. "He dun slap tinna umba too!" one declared.

They quickly left when we heard crashing footsteps coming from behind me, and three large swamp giants appeared. The giants just stood over me for a moment, then one blurted "I don't remember eating him!"

His comment made the other two laugh out loud, so much so, that they rolled on the ground, holding their noses. "What is that supposed to mean?" I thought.

"Go ahead, you scum," I yelled at them. "Eat me. I hope you all choke!"

The giant reached out with his finger, and I hesitated, but grabbed onto it anyway with both hands. He lifted me out of the murk and sat me down before the three of them. My face dripped with slime. "Well," I declared. "Do your worst!"

"I already did," the swamp giant declared. "That hole be our latrine!"

At that point, I kind of wished they had eaten me.

***

Entry 27

Not many people realize this, but dungeon exploring is perilous work and requires that you carry a lot of extra underpants. I kid you not. Try walking into a room when a half-decomposed lich jumps out of the dark and into your face. Whether you fight him or not, I guarantee there's a mess in your trousers!

I've seen the bravest warriors, the most powerful wizards, and even cunning thieves, like myself, take their share of the treasure and wiggle-walk to some corner for a quick change. One time, I got hired by an old fool of a wizard named Nilrem, to escort him through the lower levels of a dungeon. I'll never forget it, because he wore a large purple hat covered with runes, which later became covered with ruins!

He was surprised in a hallway by a single rat; not even a big one! Apparently, he doesn't like them. He screamed like a banshee and jumped into a corner hollering "Kill it! Kill it!" I dispatched the small pest with a quick stab of Magurk. A hatless Nilrem slowly crept out of the shadows, quivering and asking "Is it dead?"

"It's dead," I responded. "Hey, where's your hat?"

"Mind your own business, thug!" he said, through clenched teeth. He blushed pretty badly and stormed ahead. I couldn't help but laugh when his shoes made squishing noises as he walked away!

Entry 28

I was once almost betrothed to a lady named Ooga Igga Egga Ogga Oge. She wasn't very attractive. As a matter of fact, I would say she looked half-goblin or something. It was a crossbow wedding, as some would call it. One night, I was feeling a bit peckish, so I had crept around the woods looking for a squirrel, or even a handful of mushrooms.

Then, I smelled it. Bacon. Its strong scent caught my attention, and my stomach couldn't handle it. Without thinking twice, I made my way towards the delicious aroma. Through some trees, I spotted a small campfire and what appeared to be a little woman holding a pan over it. "I could just put her to sleep and take it," I thought to myself. I searched through my pouches 'till I found a small bit of Sleeping Dust.

As I cautiously moved forward, I stepped into a noose that was lying on the ground. A trap! Cursed bacon! As the rope wrapped around my ankle and lifted me in the air, the Sleep Dust flew from my hand, and I went through it. I don't know what happened after that, because I was sleeping like a baby.

When I finally woke up, I was on my knees with my hands tied behind my back facing the smoldering fire. To my right, was a skinny little halfling named Rugfoot, and on my left, was an orc, named Moe Hawk. Standing before us, in a shoddy, stained wedding dress, was one of the ugliest women I had ever seen. If she had more than two teeth, I couldn't tell! Her mottled black hair and flavedo skin tone was only outdone by her mangy, braided armpit hair, which probably ran a hotel for fleas. Apparently, the three of us fell for the old "snag-a-husband" trap, because standing next to her was her large, homely father, holding the most brutal looking crossbow I had ever laid eyes on.

"Howdy boys, my name is Cletus Bucketbow, and this is my daughter, Ooga Igga Egga Ogga Oge," he stated, then paused, looking at each of our faces. "One of you lucky fellers is gonna be my new son-in-law!"

Being the most handsome of the group, I got a sickening feeling in my gut. When she gave me a wink, I turned my head and threw up all over Rugfoot. "Save that for the honeymoon!" Cletus shouted at me, pointing the crossbow at my face.

"Now, which one of you boys is willin' to step up and marry my little princess?" he shouted, spittle flying.

I looked at Moe the Orc, and he was crying. I was almost in tears, myself, when I heard Rugfoot shout, "I'll do it! She's beautiful!"

Ooga Igga Egga Ogga Oge brushed past Moe Hawk and me, nearly knocking us over...with her smell. The half-goblin gal ran over to the little halfling and gave him a big hug. That night, Moe Hawk and I were best men at the wedding. We feasted on bacon and had a splendid time. The happy couple would soon be enjoying their honeymoon, but it was Moe Hawk and me who were counting our lucky stars!

Entry 29

I went to a nearby temple to see Derek the Cleric about a skin rash that I had gotten from roaming some sewers and clearing out giant rat infestations. I thought my ailment was bad, but it turns out the service at this Ready Bled was even worse! First, I was in the waiting room for over an hour-and-a-half. A guy with most of his arm cut off came in and got to see the cleric right away; totally cutting in front of me!

Ten minutes later, the guy came out with his arm grown back. Seeing that, I thought it would be worth the wait, so I read a few more of the outdated sports scrolls lying about. However, it was a full twenty minutes before the clerical assistant took me back into a temple room where, again, I had to wait. Ugh. I couldn't read any of the scrolls anymore; too many ads. Just as I started to snooze, Derek knocked on the door and walked in. "So, a thief who couldn't sneak around bacteria and got trapped with an uncomfortable rash, eh?"

I rolled my eyes, then lifted up my tunic and showed him. He sucked air through his teeth while shaking his head. "Hmmm...this is a special case," he warned. He opened up a chest of vials and bottles and pulled out a large jar of a yellowish cream.

"Can't you just pray or cast a spell or something?" I asked.

Derek just smirked at me and said, "Do you want the cream or not?"

I couldn't take the itch much longer, so I took it and walked out into the waiting room where I applied the foul smelling cream. It burned like crazy and nearly cleared the place out!

After three days of bearing with the odor and the itching, the rash finally went away. I later found out that Derek the Cleric wasn't in the accepted cleric list on my Crimson Roof Guild Health Insurance plan, so he wasn't allowed to use a healing or cure disease spell. It turns out, the only one on my plan was five days travel from where I was at. Things got worse when I found out what my deductible would be. At this point I began to wonder who was the real thief!

Entry 30

I was sitting in Dish 'n' Dirt Tavern, in the city of Amscray, when I heard the news of a barbarian warlord named Uno Dose who had taken over a nearby outpost. Apparently, he hired a motley crew of misfits who had been bullying Amscray's citizens for a while. I wasn't going to get involved, because I was only in town to restock my dwindling potion supply. I was down to a half a Healing Potion, one drop of strength, and a full bottle of acid.

The local constable approached me and a few others, begging us to take Uno Dose out. I was going to say no, until he laid a large sack of gold on the table. "When the mission is completed," he instructed. "Split this with whomever has the courage to join you."

A muscular dwarf, named Logtoss, stepped from the shadows and said, "Count me in!"

A few others stepped up too, so I figured I might as well. All of these guys looked tough as nails, and I needed those potions, anyway. It was only a few hours travel by foot to the outpost, and we were able to sneak up to the door, thanks to the diminishing sunlight. I picked the lock for the fighters, and they slew the guards pretty easily. It wasn't long before the whole gang was in an all-out brawl somewhere in the middle of the outpost.

I was just about to stab a cross-eyed orc shaman, when Uno Dose stepped into the battle and started bashing heads. The barbarian was in full rage mode and chopped one of my lot in half. I thought he'd have the upper hand until Logtoss crushed the enraged barbarians knee to a pulp with his war hammer. Our party's archer, Swatfly, was picking off the uncoordinated minions one-by-one, so I knew the battle was going our way.

The shaman tried casting some spell, but I tackled the grimy creature and disrupted his efforts. Uno Dose shouted something to the orc shaman, but I was keeping him from responding. The shaman struck my face with his mace until I let go, then he ran over to his boss, who was down on one knee fighting off the now wounded Logtoss. The orc reached into his pouch and handed the barbarian a potion. Uno Dose bit off the cork and gulped it down quickly. Through my swollen eye, I could see the orc shaman turn to me with a big grin and wiggle his finger in the "come fight with me" way.

I wiggled my index finger back at him in the "tut tut" way and pointed behind him. He paused and looked back to see Uno Dose's guts splashing out onto the floor. He had drunk the entire vial of acid that I stuck into the shaman's bag, while removing the healing potion, which I now drank.

The shaman's smile dropped into a frown, and then he dropped his mace before trying to run and slipped on his former master's gut ooze. That's the moment he was "owstruck;" that's a word I made up for when an arrow from our archer goes through your head.

Entry 31

When I was a teen, I went to school with a pimple-faced halfling, named Piddlepeck Mudpants. He was small, ate his boogers, and wrote short stories for fantasy books. He was incredibly book smart, and he would help me with subjects where I tended to struggle. Like most oddball brainiacs, he got razzed a bunch by the so-called "cool kids," but I felt sorry for him, so I shadowed him to make sure he didn't get harassed.

A snobby kid, named Tripp Makimfall, would torment poor Piddlepeck whenever I wasn't around. Tripp was a local constable's son, so he thought he could get away with anything, and usually did. One day, Tripp and his crew of tough kids dragged Piddlepeck into an outhouse and were planning to dunk him in. The problem was that I was in there, so they kept banging on the door and yelling for me to hurry up.

I peered out of the moon hole, saw who it was and what was happening, and yelled out "Give me a second!"

Without hesitation, I grabbed a wooden bucket that was in the corner of the outhouse. It was filled to the brim with grim, as I like to say, and I opened the door and dumped it over Tripp's head. His crew was so stunned that they didn't pay attention when I grabbed little Piddlepeck and ran off into the woods. The halfling always helped me after that. I didn't mind helping. I couldn't stand Makimfall or any of his friends.

I'm glad I helped the little guy back then, because later in life, I was caught up in a shady deal with an anti-paladin who, surprise, surprise, double-crossed me.

I was pretty much surrounded by his orc minions when a small fighter appeared out of nowhere. His little dragon skull helmet was a dead giveaway...it was the legendary Dragonbeast the Devastator! This hero of the region was covered with magically enhanced weaponry and attribute enhancement equipment. He was feared by many, and for a good reason, he was a killing machine.

I watched, in awe, as Dragonbeast crushed all of the orc hordes without breaking a sweat, and then tore the anti-paladins head off with his bare hands. "This would be neat for a story, wouldn't it?" he said to me in a squeaky, off-key voice.

"Is that you, Piddlepeck?" I asked, as I knelt down to shake his hand.

"That's right," he replied, as he used the freshly torn off head for a stool, its mouth still moving in a nervous twitch.

I couldn't believe ole' Mudpants had become such an amazing warrior! I asked him how he had made the transition. "It was all because I stumbled across these magic bracers! They grant you super strength!" he revealed, in a sort of whisper voice. "Years after graduation, I was studying to be a cleric's apprentice at the local guild when I bumped into Tripp and his gang. They chased me for awhile, but I hid in the wood's by Leper's Lake."

"That's a desperate move," I responded. "Even a powerful cleric would have a hard time curing the folks who roam around there!"

"I know," he responded. "But I was desperate, and I knew Tripp wouldn't follow me in there."

Piddlepeck removed his helmet and started to polish the blood off his glasses. "I came across a corpse of a fallen fighter. He was loaded up with magical items, including these bracers! I removed everything that looked valuable from the body with some long sticks and tied the pile together. I dragged the pile to my teacher, and he did a whole bunch of spells and chants over them. After a week, he declared them safe, and I got to keep all of it!"

"That's way cool!" I replied, impressed with how things worked out and how Piddlepeck seemed to adjust to his new lifestyle. "But I wonder whatever happened to Tripp and his gang?"

"Do you want to see," Piddlepeck asked, as he started to open his backpack.

"No, thank you," I frowned.

Suddenly, I was very glad I was on this halfling's good side.

€ntry 32

Does anybody else love dice games? I sure do. I used to play all sorts of them with a pal of mine who owned a nacho stand in Shallowditch. He was a dark elf, named El Rick. Once in a while, his cook, Moongum would play also. Most of the time, it was just El Rick and I fighting over the rules.

Whenever you play these multi-sided dice games, there's always some rules lawyer, like El Rick, trying to undermine your victories. I don't think he ever trusted me. Maybe it was my dark cloak or my tendency to slip loaded dice onto the game board when he was distracted by customers.

El Rick wasn't any better, though. He would have Moongum stand behind me holding a giant spike hammer. Moongum would mutter things like "just try it," or "Skullcrusher is so hungry!"

I didn't let this bother me, though; I loved playing and eating the nachos. Moongum never saw me pinch out of his tip jar when he'd get behind the counter to serve customers. That's how I paid for my meals there, most of the time!

€ntry 33

Shatterdrum, the Lounge Lizardman, was the worst bard in all four of the Unremembered Realms. His off-key singing made you want to stick knives in your ears to ease the pain. Of course, he didn't realize how awful he was. I once used him to fleece unknowing audiences. We toured around the realms for quite a bit, until he figured out my game.

Every night, as he'd play and sing, I'd hold up a sign with the words "Pay, and he'll stop!" He thought the sign I'd never show him read "Encore." The audience would throw coins, jewels, and even magical items. When the pile got big enough, I'd tell him to stop, "Leave them wanting more," I'd say. So we'd collect the loot and slither out the back.

Well, one night, while playing in the gambling town of Hollerbluff, one of my earplugs exploded during one of his yodels, and that was enough for me. Oh well, it was fun while it lasted. The last I heard of Shatterdrum, he got employed by a human fighter named Liveraunchie, a Captain of the Guard at Lhentil Keep. I guess he plays his music for captured enemies, and from what I heard, his songs make the prisoners sing, and not just the blues!

Entry 34

Not long after graduating from the Crimson Roof Thieves Guild, an elf classmate of mine and I were hired to tag along with some adventuring team to pick locks and whatnot. On the east side of the Province of Rippenwind, was a small dungeon that got overrun by goblins and their surprisingly powerful Fangknight leader, Kildemal.

The whole thing turned out to be a little more than we expected. Our party had made some progress in our run-in with Kildemal. He almost lived up to his name, but my classmate, Spex, and I managed to slip out of the battle with only a few cuts and burns. As we ran through the hallways, seeking the way out, Spex whined and complained as he was wont to do. "How come you didn't use your poison arrows?", "You sure were useless back there!", and "Didn't you read any of your guild textbooks?!"

Spex was a real book worm, and to his credit, he did know the rules. The problem was, we lived in the real world, not some fanta-syland described in a book. A thief had to be smart, but also crafty and able to seize any opportunity. Kind of like when I raided Kildemal's treasure chest, while everyone was fighting. Spex didn't even notice my jingling pockets as I ran. Or course, how could he? He never shut his yap the whole time we were running!

"Your clothes are too bright. Your dagger's too small. You've got to learn to be quiet," he droned on.

Then, out of nowhere, a trap sprung out from under our feet. Spex's chatter distracted me, so I never saw the pressure plate on the floor that activated the trap. We fell twenty feet and hit the bare cement with a thud. "Ow!" Spex shouted loudly. "Why didn't you see that trap!?"

I knew I cracked a rib, because I was short of breath and my chest hurt. But, Spex's leg was all twisted up, so I knew he was going to be a load to carry. He sat back against a wall and caught his breath. At that moment, we could hear a goblin patrol coming down some nearby corridor. "Got a plan, genius?" Spex looked at me like I should have an answer. "Or, are you still the mid-grade level rogue who slept through all the key classes?"

I didn't say anything, but dug through my pockets, until I found two rings that had been in Kildemal's treasure chest. They both bore a spider symbol on the top, so I figured they might be helpful in this situation. I slipped mine on and walked over to the elf. "Here," I told him. "Use this."

"I don't need your help, underclassman," he sneered. "I've read all the manuals. I know what to do."

I could hear the goblins voices getting louder with each passing moment. "Come on fool," I whispered. "Listen. I'm sorry I poured a Cause Baldness Potion in your soup in the cafeteria."

He straightened his toupee and pushed up his thick glasses, until his eyes were as large as saucers. "What makes you think I couldn't kill you right now, myself?" he said holding up his dagger.

I'd just about had enough, so I knocked the dagger from his hand and stuffed the ring into his palm. I leaned forward and whispered into his ear, "Because I used to catch you copying off my test papers, faker!"

The goblins voices were even louder now, so I gave up and ran to the outer wall and started climbing straight up it. The Spider Climbing ring worked! Spex kept yelling, like a fool, so I just left. I heard the goblins shouting as I listened to the bald elf yelling, "I'll get you for this!"

I didn't give it a second thought after that, until now. I mean, what are the odds of an insane person like that escaping, only to hunt me down someday for their blood-curdling revenge...oh, wait, that's a story for another time...

Entry 35

As my party traveled through a swampy region of the Unremembered Realms, known as Widowsmarsh, we came upon a patrol of lizardmen who had been raiding local caravans. Our barbarian fighter dove into the group head-on and started bashing their skulls with his war hammer. I always found Smashemflat the perfect name for him. He just hated surprises.

It wasn't long before Knuckleflip, our Wizard, was casting some oddly helpful spell at the horrible creatures. Three of the lizardmen started in for us back three, the cleric, Fumblegums the Undentured, the samurai Musashi, and me. I was notching an arrow, as the lizardmen hit us head on. Musashi was taken off guard and did a big backswing, trying to slice two of them at once. He fumbled his blade, and it lopped my left hand off.

As I screamed and started to pass out, I saw Smashemflat running our way, swinging his hammer and yelling his battle cry, "Mash their brains, Hammerkiss!"

When I woke up, Fumblegums was standing over me, smiling. "What happened?" I asked, groggily.

"I fithed your hand!" the toothless cleric said proudly, in his weird lisp. "I found thum' thpare partths!"

I looked at my hand and noticed the green, scaly fingers and sharp nails. "I have a Meld thpell that I've modified for healing," Fumblegums said happily. "Hope you don't mind being my tesht patient."

I chased him for half a mile with my dagger, but the old codger actually could run. "Thtop!" he yelled.

The others ran after us, trying to stop me, so I decided to chase Musashi around with the dagger. I miss happy days like that. Those were good times.

Entry 36

I was waiting in line at an equipment shop, and this hipster druid tried cutting in front of me. First off, I hate druids, and second, this one bumped into me, while pushing ahead. "Who made this floppy hat goofball king of the store," I wondered.

What made it even worse, was there are six lanes and only two are ever actually open, so, unless you come early in the morning, you're going to get stuck in the slow lane. It is always the one with the peppy clerk who is trying to get people to sign up for their frequent customer programs.

I tapped the druid on the shoulder and gave a pretty harsh "ahem" sound. He turned around quickly, and I received a stern rebuke. "I am Doopercap the Magnificent! Away with thee, knave!"

He called me worse names after I rammed my knee into his stomach and daggered his hand to the floor. What made matters worse that day, was I found out the magic beans I bought weren't magic at all! Note to self: Stab Robbie the Thief.

Entry 37

I got hired by a wealthy druid, named Toopfish, to help him take out his sworn enemy in a nearby castle. I can't stand druids, most of the time, but this one said the magic word: gold! He, like most druids, was into that au natural stuff; in other words: no bathing. If anyone smelled like a toilet, it was Toopfish.

They are all way into recycling too. Toopfish would make hats out of his old underpants and tea filters from his old socks. I took care not to drink any of his "refreshments."

Toopfish had been hunting down his enemy for a while. His name was Tubbring, and he was hoping to kill off all the races with his creation of carnivorous hybrid plants. Toopfish hired fighters, rangers, and a cleric, and most of them died by being devoured by the genetic monstrosities of nature. Just a few of us remained when we finally managed to find Tubbring hiding in his greenhouse laboratory. The battle soon became quite intense. At one point, both druids started using their armpit sweat as components for their spells. That was just about it for me, so I decided to leave. But, not before I discreetly snagged a couple of pouches off Toopfish's robe, while he was distracted. I was bound to collect my fee, win or lose.

While our fighters were distracted by Genus Guytrap plants and the druids were now into fisticuffs, I opened the pouches to take a peek at Toopfish's stash. One was full of seeds, while the other held dung. Why was I not surprised, the druid would drone on and on about rare animal manure! As I hid under a lab table, trying to figure a way out of the place, the two druids came crashing through the table, knocking me over and spilling the pouches contents everywhere.

Tubbring was no lightweight, and he was practically sitting on top of me exchanging blows with Toopfish. The blubbery druid received a stab in the backside from Magurk, as I tried to get him off me. "Mehgurkkk!" he shouted as he tumbled away, with Toopfish in hot pursuit.

Toopfish and a remaining fighter used this as an opportunity to jump on the wounded Tubbring and finish him off. That's when I realized that Toopfish would notice his missing pouches! I quickly looked among the mess and saw that the seeds and manure I spilled were now mixed in with the evil druids very own seeds.

I randomly grabbed handfuls of seeds and dung, stuffing them into the pouches as quickly as I could. "Great job, rogue!" shouted the smiling druid, as he came over to help me stand up.

While he helped me stand, I gently put his pouches back. "Never had a doubt, Toopfish," I replied.

He rewarded me and the remaining fighter handsomely and we parted ways. The last time I heard about him was from a news scroll that I picked up about a year later when I was visiting the area. The headline read: "Druid missing. Man-Eating Plant Farm Closed Until Further Investigation."

Entry 38

I was traveling, one night, through the town of Neverspring, when I spotted a flyer up on a community board advertising "The Realms Most Haunted House!" I was broke and hungry, so I figured I could eliminate a few undead and possibly find a few coins in the old place. If there was one thing I knew, haunted houses, castles, and graveyards were great places to find treasure. Most people avoid these places like the plague, as well they should! Some of the dead probably passed away, because of it.

It's hard for most to kill ghosts, but I knew my dagger, Magurk, was magical, and the undead are easily vanquished with enchanted items. By the time I got there, it had gotten dark, so I snuck up to a back door and tiptoed in. I heard a woman scream and some people yelling, so I figured the ghosts were attacking some other treasure seekers. I bounded into the room, quickly, and stabbed the first ghost I saw. With a shriek, it crumpled to the floor. I jumped on it again, with Magurk, but it caught my wrist. "Quit stabbing me, fool!" it yelled out at me.

That's when I noticed all the blood. That's weird, I thought, I never knew ghosts bled. Seconds later I was surrounded by other ghosts and some zombies, or what appeared to be. "We're not dead; we're actors! This building is a fun house!"

"Are you sure?" I asked, raising my dagger up to them, holding them all back. "Yes!" they all screamed at once. I turned and ran. It was so dark that I knocked over a box near the back door and it spilled a bunch of coins on the floor. I scooped up as much as I could before the others appeared in full chase mode. I must have run three miles before I finally lost them. They kept screaming "Come back!" Then, something about a tip or donation box or something. Why would I tip them? They were trying to kill me!

It may not have been what I thought it was, but it did prove my theory correct – haunted houses are an excellent way to make some quick coin.

Entry 39

Have you ever encountered a harpy? I have. Three actually. They killed off a couple of my companions and hauled me off to their nests. Apparently, they were full because they didn't kill or eat me. I think the real reason they kept me alive was to complain. Harpies love to whine, nag, and moan about their lives.

They used me to clean their nest, throw out trash, and give a "pedi" to their razor sharp claws. I heard all the gossip while they had their hair up in human bone curlers. I didn't care how their bird brain boyfriends treated them or why they'd never bird call them after a date.

"All men are pigs!" they'd say, or "Why doesn't he invite me to a game with his buddies?" Then the tears. Ugh. They'd cry on my shoulders and hug me (usually puncturing me somewhere), before harping on about all the pressures of being a modern half-human half-bird cannibal.

Surprisingly, they let me go after three weeks. Apparently, I lost enough weight to where they didn't think I was worth eating. They asked me to bird call them, but I never will. Those chicks were nuts.

Entry 40

I was walking along a muddy road on my way to pick up some food rations in the nearby town of Swindleton. It had been raining quite heavily, so I should have tried to wait it out, but I'd been living on wild fruit and berries the last couple of days. I heard some splashes in the distance behind me, so I turned around and saw a beautiful travel wagon being pulled by a pair of horses.

Quickly pulling out my magical Hat of Disguising, I put it on and willed myself into the look of an old man. I stepped to the side of the road and arched my back a little. Sympathy could get me a warm ride for the rest of the journey! I raised my thumb and smiled, pathetically, as the wagon sped past and splashed a bunch of mud all over me.

"Get off the road, you old fool!" came a voice from inside the wagon.

I could also hear a woman's laughter come from inside the carriage. The chauffeur of the wagon just hung his head, as he led them off. They rode off quickly, leaving me standing there wiping mud from my face. I took the hat off and stuffed it back into my pack. It must not have been an hour later when I spotted the wagon again. The rain had reduced to a drizzle by the time I approached. It appeared that one of the wheels had come off and the chauffeur was struggling to fix it.

It was evident that they did not recognize me, because I was no longer in disguise. "Excuse me, sir," the driver inquired. "Could you give me a hand? I have an important speaker who needs to be in Swindleton in about five hours."

I looked inside the warm, dry wagon and saw the man who had taunted me earlier. He looked back at me with a contemptuous smile. His small set blue eyes never blinked as he leaned forward to speak down to me. "My name is Turgid Bragswagger," he stated. "I've got an important lecture to give at the Constable Convention in Swindleton."

He could probably tell that I wasn't impressed or that I'd never heard of him before. "Listen, chum. I'm a big deal around here. I am the greatest detective in all of Cloverose! Lawmen from all the realms will be at the convention to hear nuggets of my wisdom!"

I didn't move. "Here," Turgid stated, pulling out a large coin purse. "Take five gold. Now help our useless chauffeur and get us back on the road."

The woman with him frowned at me as I took the gold, I grinned back at her as she turned away in disgust. It only took about ten minutes of fixing the wagon before it was ready to go. "Thank you, sir," the chauffeur said, as he reached out to shake my hand.

When he reached his hand out, I placed the five gold in his palm. "No," I stated. "Thank you. Now scram."

With my other hand, I gave a slight reveal of my dagger, and he went wide-eyed. I gave him a wink and a shush as he trotted off down the road. Moments later, the two passengers were tied to a tree by the side of the road. "You're going to pay for this, you dog!"

the man spat at me, as he struggled with his ropes. "You had better run; there's a whole convention full of lawmen who will hunt you down!"

"That's right, mongrel," his female companion shouted. "We know your face."

I smiled and pulled out my Hat of Disguising, placing it on my head. Within moments of studying his face, I transformed my appearance so that I looked just like him. "So will they," I laughed as I threw his coin purse into my pack. "They are not going to like what you have to say at all."

"You can't take my place! They know who I am! They'll not fall for some buffoons hat trick! I have a reputation!" he screamed as I turned away.

I paused, then turned around, "You're going to have a new one, now. The con is on!"

News traveled fast of the crazy detective speaker who gave one of the most incendiary speeches in the Constable Convention's history. Not only did the Realms now notorious detective spend most of the time insulting the intelligence of the audience, but it turns out that he also robbed the rooms of most of the lawmen while they were having brunch right before his lecture.

Entry 41

I'd been traveling with Welhoff the Minotaur for about three months promoting his snake oil business. The minotaur had taken an old family recipe for curing constipation and repackaged it as a weight-loss energy potion he called Flying Bull. You get an energy boost (the urge to fly to an outhouse) and lose weight naturally (answering nature's call).

Being that Welhoff was a large, muscular half-bull and half-man, it made it hard for him to work directly with the people. The daunting creature wouldn't hurt a fly (unless provoked), but nevertheless, people tend to judge a book by its cover. One day he saw me working a crowd with one of my sleight-of-hand scams and asked me if I'd help him push his product.

We did well for a while, even experimenting with different products. We tried cold medicine for frost giants, skunk deodorants, and even a sun tan lotion for vampires. None of these worked too well, so we would get run out of town before too long. I couldn't tell if the suntan lotion worked or not, though; the vampires never returned.

Our snake oil days ended when we set up our display in the blink town of Underpyle. Mayor Podunk, an overweight dwarf with a bad eye twitch, stopped by our wagon to check out our wares. "This will give people energy?" he asked.

"Sure," I replied. "You'll fly like you have wings. As a matter of fact, you'll go like a goose."

"Give me a half-dozen bottles then," he requested. "They are for my Dragonslayer Knights. These energy potions will come in handy for their battle tomorrow with Blowback, the Skull Crunching dragon of Darkenbleak."

My eyes grew wide, as the six Dragonslayers approached, each grabbing a vial from me. These knights were gigantic and wore heavy plate mail armor. I could almost feel their swords slice through me, just by glancing at them! "Listen fellas," I started to confess, but I was quickly cut off by a knight's blade at my throat.

"What are you saying fool," the angered knight's voice echoed in his helmet. "Are these a scam?!"

I deftly stepped back and put my hands up. Within seconds, Welhoff was outside of the tent and into the knight's face. "Back off, human!" he said, gruffly. "Our product is top-notch. If this won't make you move, nothing will!"

The standoff quieted down, and Welhoff and I collected our gold. We packed up our stuff that night and split town. From the rumors we heard, the knights drank our potion right before the big battle and things kind of went to pot. Blowback ended up using their heavy plate mail as dinner plate mail. I guess they couldn't close the back flaps and the dragon peeled the armor off like we would a shrimp's shell.

The problem was that they were still digesting our potion as he gobbled them down. Blowback flew around in a rage relieving himself and covering the city of Underpyle. Even poor Mayor Podunk got double-covered and smothered. The whole town was steaming...mad.

Wellhoff and I decided to part ways after that and that was all right by me; I was getting tired of pushing a crappy product. I guess Welhoff became quite the salesman after that and rebranded the product as a laxative; I suppose he's making piles himself now...of money.

Entry 42

There was an elderly dignitary that needed armed security as he traveled from the town of Miftenmad to Neverspring. The old man was quite nervous about the trip and was paying quite a bit, so I joined the party as a scout. I'm not a very good scout, but he didn't know that. It's not that I don't see things, but I just don't care enough to pay attention. I didn't even notice the "Forbidden Zone" signs that were all over the shortcut that I recommended.

Needless to say, it wasn't long before we were locked in combat with a large group of bandits trying to raid our caravan. I have to admit; they were a tough lot. Both of our groups had wiped each other out. I was cut up badly and crawling my way towards their corpses to search for treasure when a boot crushed my hand. "Is that you cousin?" a familiar voice asked.

I looked up, and there he was, my ugly cousin Stabbinal. He was in rough shape but still able to stand. I smiled and gave a weak wave, as he pushed me over onto my back. "Long time no see, eh?" he sneered happily.

"How's Auntie Hogbreath?" I asked, with a sneer.

He just frowned at me, while pulling out his dagger. "Let's just say this," he said as he knelt down. "You're going to meet the same fate!"

With that said, he thrust his dagger into my side, well, tried to anyway. The blade hit a couple of glass vials that I had hid under my cloak. "Well, well, well," he said amusingly. "A refreshing little treat!"

He pulled them out of my pocket. It was a vial containing a healing potion and a vial of painful death poison. He held them up, smiling. "I have an idea!" he held up the healing vial and almost took a drink. "Wait a minute..." he paused. "If I know you, cousin, you switched the poison and the healing. It's the oldest trick in the book.

He uncorked the healing vial and poured it down my throat. I winced, choked, reached up for him and pretended to die. He laughed out loud, uncorked the poison bottle and drank it in one gulp. "Feeling any better, cousin?" I said, as I stood up.

He looked at me with a shocked expression as the empty vial slipped from his fingers. "Wha..." he mumbled, as he fell to his knees. "I swiped the healing vial off the party's cleric right before this battle, Stabbinal," I smirked. "I didn't have time to switch out the labels."

As he gave up the ghost, I gathered up all the valuables, loaded the wagon, and headed out for the next town. I'd like to say things went smoothly, but I didn't read the next group of signs either. From what I encountered, it should have read "Angry Cannibal Giants!"

Entry 43

Hotfoot was a wild elf who adventured with me a few times. His ability to ruin a surprise attack was only balanced out by his handiness with a flaming arrow. I don't know how many orc caravans have got it out for this guy, but I guess there is quite a few. What I don't get is that he burns them for fun and never actually cares about the loot. That's an elf for you.

One night, just for fun, I snuck into an orc camp and painted bullseyes all over the wagons, orcs, and even their pack mules. When they hit the trail the next day, Hotfoot and I had a blast using our bows to "hit the targets." Whoever got the most points would be declared the winner and had to pay for the other one's dinner.

I'd say we were both lucky, because I happened to outshoot him for once, which was fortunate for me. It was fortunate for him too, because while he was sleeping, I painted a bullseye on his back, in case I lost the wager.

Entry 44

I returned to my hometown apartment one day to drop off some goods, and I stepped over a stack of mail collecting dust on the floor. Inside most of them were some curses, IOU inquiries, and some letters from mom.

The majority of them were the usual death threats or pleads for money, but one I found was a thank you note. It read:

"Dear son, thanks for the birthday gift of a treasure map. It has paid off. I hired a small team of adventurers, and we explored the lost caves of Dankmud. The fat and lazy dragon who inhabited the cave had eaten all of his minions and was pretty much left weak and defenseless. I am now living a posh lifestyle on an island that I won't mention. I put up some 'dead or alive' reward posters with a sketch of you on them before I left. It's a decent sized amount, so travel safely," Love, Mom."

I had bought the map for mom from Robbie the Thief thinking this would at least be the end of the backstabbing, old hag. Leave it to that traitor to sell me an honest-to-goodness actual treasure map! Note to self: Run Robbie over with a horse drawn wagon.

Entry 45

Every year, I am required to attend the Annual Thieves Guild meeting in Neverspring. It is probably the lamest get together of all time. I'm always stuck talking to the higher-ups, so I have to be polite. I know better, though, because this group is nothing but a bunch of back stabbers.

One year broke all the records of tedium, though. They brought in Nimblefist the Braggard to be our featured speaker. The lame windbag brought a rolling tray full of scrolls and commenced to drone on and on using empowering points, lectures on scold calling, and ever so annoying back door-to-door assassin techniques.

The entertainment was atrocious, too. It was a group of druid/bards who sang about rainbows and something about putting flour in their hair...who does that crap?! How would you even comb it then? I felt like throwing a dagger through their hair.

The only highlight of the evening was all of the pickpocketing going on. I always stuff my pockets with White War Elephant gifts. Those are always good for a laugh. I was pickpocketed so much that I don't think I ever held the same item twice. I did manage to steal what I thought was a cool looking treasure map off Robbie the Thief.

It turned out not to be a treasure map at all, but a piece of one of the singing druids tie-dyed robes...with a fresh blood stain on it. Note to self: Let Robbie the Thief live another week.

Entry 46

I was holed up for the winter season in a small house just outside the city of Amscray. I had rented a small room from an old crone, named Gabenyap. I thought she had a crush on me, because she would always follow me around and sniff at me. But, she fed me well. I have to admit, I put on a few pounds of winter weight.

She was kind of eccentric. She would look through my window at night, while licking her lips. One night, I peeked over my blanket to see if she had left and she had her bulbous eye smashed up against the glass. I could still see the eye print on it the next day!

One extra cold day, I woke up to find her two older, uglier sisters had come for a visit! "He's not very plump," one said while looking me over. "You haven't been feeding him well."

"He was a toothpick, Naginhag," Gabenyap replied.

"Speaking of toothpicks, did you remember to get some?" the other sister asked.

"Yes, Flavedina, of course!" she answered. Then, they all gathered around me, sniffing and smiling. "We have a special surprise for you!"

They guided me into what I had thought was Gabenyap's cellar. In the center of the room, was a giant black cauldron. "It's a nice spa for you to relax in!" Flavedina said. "I hope you enjoy it."

The other two giggled and I reluctantly agreed to try it out. By this time, I had figured out what was going on. "After this, we'll have a big lunch," Hagitha cheered. All three began laughing.

"Sure," I replied. "Just let me change into my swim trunks."

After putting on shorts, I came out and lowered my body into the hot water of the spa; it felt pretty good. "This is nice," I told them. "Why are there carrot and potato chunks in here?"

"To soften the skin," Gabenyap replied. "It's an old beauty secret."

The witches must have gone senile or something; none of these crones was an old beauty. "It sure smells good in here," I stated. "I bet it tastes good!"

After I had taken a small sip, all three gathered around the pot, with their mouths watering. "Here," I said. "Let me stir this around and you can try it yourselves."

I sank myself up to my neck and moved my body around, just to make sure all the ingredients were just right. All three leaned over the pot and started taking large sips from the cauldron. They all started shrieking with delight...then there was just screaming and clutching their own throats. They all began to do some incantation, but they never finished their spells because they all fell over dead.

I climbed out of the cauldron and dried off. I removed the empty bottles of poison from my shorts and went and changed. I stayed warm, dry, and fed for the rest of the winter, thanks to several dwarves who lived just down the road.

Entry 47

One of the strangest things that I ever saw in my travels was King Smudley's Vagabones Circus. Apparently, this looney cleric thought he could make a few coins by raising the dead and performing feats in a three ring sideshow. It was a failure on so many levels, that I actually followed it around for a bit, just to watch it implode.

First of all, King Smudley wasn't a king. His name was Butterfield Smudpimple. He was a novice cleric who kind of thought of himself as a genius. "Let's fleece the chumps!" he'd yell out at the start of every show.

I told him to pep talk the performers before the show, not during the show, when the audience was sitting on the bleachers. If the public decided to stay, at that point, they got to see a zombie tamer try to stick his head into the zombie's mouth. Let's just say that never worked out too well. My job was to go in and kill the zombie after it tore into the performer's brain. On the plus side, we always used the newly deceased performer as the zombie for the following week's show.

In an amazing feat that even I was impressed with, King Smudley got over two dozen zombie clowns stuffed into one wagon. When they pulled this out to the audience, it seemed like the undead would never stop pouring out of it. Kids kind of freaked out at the zombies done up in clown makeup. It was a little disturbing, to say the least. But, the clincher usually ended up being when one of the parent's recognized the zombie as a friend or relative. You see, King Smudley's zombie clowns often took off after their victims, so he needed a fresh batch for every town. The fool didn't want to deal with hauling zombies through checkpoints, so he raised the dead at local cemeteries before each show.

The last night I was there, the local cleric's guild came in and busted up the act, turning the undead, bashing skulls, and finally arresting poor Smudpimple. Well, the self-proclaimed King of Entertainment would have been proud to know that I managed to rescue the money box before sneaking off into the woods...where I just happened to meet the priest who paid me the reward for turning him in.

Entry 48

Just outside of Lhentil Keep, was a small eatery known as the Baglunch Café. Every meal there was the Chef's Surprise. You never knew what you were going to get; hence the name. One particular day kind of sticks out in my mind. When I sat down at my usual outside table, I opened the bag and noticed a small bomb with the wick almost completely burned away. I quickly picked it out and threw it over my shoulder, without even really thinking. Luckily, nobody important got hurt, just a local druid who happened to catch the bomb as he was out for a walk.

This trick was obviously the work of a fellow assassin, named Low Key. He was really good at pranks. The only problem was that they were so deadly. He hadn't liked me, since I tricked him into believing in the global swarming hoax. Low Key must have bought fifty pounds of netting and covered his entire house with it. It was all because I told him I had snuck into a druidic council and they made the determination that, in less than six months, the entire Unremembered Realms would be covered with insects.

He never left his house for the whole six months. Suffice to say, he wasn't too happy with me, especially when I roared with laughter in his face.

As I sat there chuckling and wiping bits of druid off me, I noticed there was still something in the bag. I carefully opened it and peered in. It was a little toy crossbow with a poison arrow tip! Low Key didn't forget to pack the toy surprise in my meal. Who says he didn't have heart? I hit the little trigger by mistake, and it sprang, shooting a tiny bolt into the angry dwarf who was sitting next to me. He was complaining to the waiter about the druid splatter in his soup, as he suddenly became quiet and fell face first into it. I got up and retrieved the little bolt. Such a cool prize!

Entry 49

One of the downsides to being a successful rogue is that you can tick off the wrong people. I've had arrows in the back, punches to the face, and have even been thrown over a cliff. But to me, the worst thing of all is living with minor curses. During my early years, I'd go on the typical dungeon raid, and sometimes, I'd have the misfortune of bumping into some evil wizard who'd get upset just because I'd stab him and try to steal his goods.

For example, one time I was at this party, and we decided to raid the Temple of Temperamental Evil. We didn't make it far, mostly because most of us were inexperienced. Right away, we encountered a low-level wizard in charge of guarding the first floor. His name was Welcome Matt; I know that because it was on a name tag pinned to his robe. It read, "Welcome, Matt."

I admired that the dungeon keepers took so much care to train their employees properly, even the undead had tags on them labeled "skeleton," "zombie," or "ghoul." I could respect a well-structured organization; it's a sign of good management. During the battle, I almost asked what kind of benefit package they offered.

As curious as I was, though, it is hard to ask questions when you are dodging lightning bolts. Matt and his minions had nearly wiped out the party before we had a chance to do anything. I directed a couple of insults his way before escaping in the shadows. That is how I received my first minor curse. Whatever jinx he placed upon me makes me now yawn whenever someone is telling me something important or meaningful to them.

I've got lots of other curses I have to endure too: Like belching at weddings, sleeping during lectures, passionately playing the "air lute" whenever I hear a song I like, breaking wind in libraries, and giving false directions to lost tourists.

I've tried to get these curses removed by other magic-users or clerics, but they all just tell me the same thing: those aren't curses, that's just you. They would go into more detail, but I couldn't hear them through all my yawning.

Entry 50

Believe it or not, I got a job as a security guard for the First Bank of Hovelhome in the Farlong Realm. I was there to snoop around, but the almost blind halfling manager, Owen Stuft, came out from the vault announcing they'd just been robbed. I punched the wall in anger, because of my bad timing, and this caught the attention of the little number cruncher.

"You look like a trustworthy sort," he said, trying to focus on my face through his thick, thick glasses. "Don't be upset; we get robbed all the time!"

"Where is your security?" I asked.

"They are in a pile out back," he answered. "They get killed all the time. Hey, do you need a job?"

"How big is the pile?" I asked.

"Three gold a day," he replied, moving me away from the window that overlooked the back of the building.

"Five," I replied.

"Four," he volleyed back, raising a gray eyebrow.

"Deal," I said. "But I get to keep the dead robber pickings."

I was there about two weeks before "the incident." Thieves would come in, threaten the tellers, and get led back into the vault where I would be using my Blending Cloak to make myself invisible. With a stab or two, I'd have another body to chuck into the now growing body pile out back. Most of them were newbie scum who didn't know their elbow from their eyebrow.

They didn't have much, but I could get a few meals paid for. I'd even treat Owen out to dinner. One day, as we sat across the street at the Stoneshoe Tavern eating lunch, Owen spotted a crowd gathering outside the bank. We quickly jumped up from our table, ran across the street, and rushed through the back door; we nearly crashed headfirst into a wild-eyed cleric.

I never got his name, but I knew from where he raised his zombie horde. Half of them were still wearing their security uniforms! "I've got all your gold and emptied your vault," he hissed at us.

As Owen stood there stammering, I held up my hands. "Hey buddy, I'm only here to make a withdrawal," I calmly stated.

"There's nothing left to withdraw, fool," he sneered at me.

"I wouldn't say that," I replied, as I withdrew my magic dagger, Magurk, from its sheath.

Within a few moments, the looney cleric was lying on the floor, gurgling, in a pool of his own blood. I bent down over his body and retrieved my belongings. The zombie horde just stood around me, waiting like lost sheep. The cleric never had a chance to give them an order, so I figured I'd try it out. "Line up along the wall," I commanded.

The zombies did the same. I turned to Owen and gave him my key to the door. "Looks like you got all your guards back, and more!"

Owen nodded. "You know, they probably don't need much," he commented. "Just a robber to eat, once in a while."

We shook hands and parted ways. The halfling had his new employees, and I had the sack of gold the cleric had collected from the bank. I was sure glad that Owen had horrible eyesight.

Entry 51

People think that being a rogue was always my first choice as a career, but it wasn't. One of my dreams, since childhood, was to be a warrior. A real stand up, take off the gloves, hack and slash orc slayer. The problem was that I didn't have the patience that I should have had in fighter training.

First off, I got a zero in armor class. Let's just say that I wasn't a "hit" with the teacher. My strength building coach said that I didn't have the fortitude, reflex, or will to stay with it. I always wondered, if I had just taken the initiative, could I have done much better?

One area in which I did excel, in though was "saving throws." Whenever in close combat, I was always able to grab my opponent and throw them over my shoulder or around my leg to make them fall. My coach said that I always scored the most "hit" points in this area.

One day, on my way to another class of brutal training, I saw a flyer up on a community board. It was for the Crimson Roof Thieves Guild. "We'll leave the light off for you," was emblazoned across the top. The rest, you might say, is the story of my life.

Entry 52

Generally, I despise animals, unless they are on my plate! So, when I got rescued by a horse, I was forced to have a slight change of heart. I had been tied with stakes to the ground in the middle of the Barrendry Desert by some unappreciative party who misunderstood my version of the word "share."

After a few days, the vultures were starting to circle above, and I had just about given up hope. Then, I felt a large shadow break the sun's rays from over me. Through blurry eyes, I looked up to see the elongated face of my rescuer...a horse. She was a medium sized, mostly brown, with a long black mane, and a white circle surrounding her right eye. She was looking pretty gaunt, like she'd been wandering the desert for a while; which, must have been difficult, considering she was weighed down with traveling supplies.

After the horse had eaten most of the food from my nearby backpack, she bit open the waterskin that my so called "friends" left just beyond my fingertips. Finally, after consuming all that she could, she started walking away. For some reason, one of my ropes got caught up around one of her hooves, and it pulled me and the sand spikes up from the ground. I was too weak to untangle myself, so she drug me along by my left arm through, what seemed like, miles of the desert.

That was okay. It was pretty slow, and I didn't have the strength to get up. I named the horse Encumbrance, because she was slow and over packed. I don't know what happened to her original owner, but I suspected the desert vultures did. Needless to say, Encumbrance and I made it back into a greener part of the realm, and I managed to find the strength from her supplies to get us both back into health after a few days.

I didn't keep good track of Encumbrance, and she wandered off again. That was okay too. I hoped that she would wander well. Little did I know this would not be our final parting.

Entry 53

Being low on food supplies, I decided to do a little fishing at Lake Caster in the Province of Elderwhelp. After walking an old path that I found, I came across a long floating pier that went about fifty feet out over the water. There, I saw an old halfling trying to catch fish with his little fishing rod. "How they biting?" I asked.

"Not so well today," he replied, moving his pole back and forth.

I peered into his empty bucket and thought I might be a help. "Hold on, old one; I'll catch us some dinner."

With that said, I took off my shirt and boots and dove into the water. And wouldn't you know it, I found two smaller sized dragonfish that had been eating all the other fish under the pier. Not wasting time, I daggered them and swam back to the surface. The old halfling was quite pleased when I dropped one into his bucket. "There you go, old timer," I smirked. "Never let a belly go empty!"

"These dragonfishes are rare!" he exclaimed. "...and I hear they can grow to the size of a small whale."

"I didn't see any that big," I said, a little relieved.

The halfling looked up at me with a serious expression. "These are just babies; I can guarantee there's a jealous momma fish around. You are either lucky, sir, or very foolish!"

"A fool with a soon to be full belly," I chuckled, patting my stomach.

"Either way, I'm grateful. My wife is an excellent cook! I should take you home for supper!"

"No thanks," I stated, knowing well that halflings are weird little creatures that will date anything! Who knows who, or to what, he was married. I might just be his lady's supper. I just smiled, waved goodbye, and went back to my camp.

The dragonfish was tasty, so I thought I'd get some more the next day. When I got to the pier, I noticed the old Halfling wasn't anywhere around, but then again, neither was the end of the pier! It was as if something had taken a huge bite out of it.

As I walked out to the end of what remained of the pier, I noticed the halfling's bucket, fishing pole, and hand floating in the newly red water. It was at that very moment that I decided to pick some fruit for breakfast.

Entry 54

The Hob Knob Tavern is not what you would call an elegant sleep. It's on the north end of Daggerfoot, which is a gathering place for the well-to-do's of the Unremembered Realms. The food they serve is top notch, not your typical gob stuffing slap-up with a leg bone of whatever. We're talking class.

Life Day, one of the Unremembered Realms biggest holidays, was rapidly approaching and I didn't want to miss out on any financial opportunities at this large of a gathering. Of course, someone like me could never make it through the front door, so I masterminded a plan to get inside.

The tavern hired me, temporarily as a waiter to serve hors d'oeuvres during the festivities. I almost felt sorry about pilfering valuables during the holiday. For most, Life Day was about setting aside differences and to bring all the peoples and creatures together in peace. For me, it was about nicking their gold and splitting town! I have to admit, though, it did warm my heart to see an elf talking to an orc and a flea-ridden kobold break bread with a halfling and his ugly girlfriend.

As the patrons removed the hors d'oeuvres from my tray, I'd remove coin pouches from their belts! I felt more like a maid than a waiter with the way I was cleaning up!

When someone in the crowd noticed their valuables missing, I purposely dumped a coin purse over by kobold representative. "Thief!" I'd point and shout, "give them their valuables back!"

The hoity-toity upper crust lost all of their composure and attacked the little creature, without even an explanation. I don't know what happened after that, because I slipped out the back. By the time the crowd figured out my scam, I'd be sitting in some off-the-wall muck 'n' crud celebrating Life Day, as I usually do, alone and plotting.

Entry 55

I was off in the woods, answering nature's call, when I heard a bunch of commotion back at my party's campsite. It was quite the conundrum, because I wasn't finished doing my business, and I was only halfway through reading the local news scroll. I hurried through the cartoon section; my favorite one is a dark comedy about a vengeful bard named "Djingo Barry."

By the time I had made it back, it was too late; it was total devastation. My party were all slain. Bibdribble the fighter, Calzone the cleric, Spotface the wizard, and Swatfly, the archer. Surrounding them was about two dozen fallen zombies. I knew right away this was the work of an evil cleric named Pandermoan.

I was just about to leave when I noticed my team usually had of all their valuables. Oh well, first come, first serve I guess, it was a shame. I liked Swatfly's Bow. It was magically accurate. That's when a thought of sheer horror came over me. I left my Cloak of Blending at the camp! I searched everywhere...but it was gone.

Needless to say, I was quite upset at this tragedy. I started pacing...and pacing, and then it hit me. There was a graveyard not too far from where I was, and Pandermoan was down a few bodies. I used my magically enhanced Speed Boots to run over there as fast as I could.

When I got to the graveyard, nothing had been disturbed. It must have been my lucky day because there were a freshly dug pit and a pile of corpses piled up next to it. The workers must have been out to lunch or something. I took a bit of rotten blood from the bodies and smeared myself up good and jumped into the pile.

It wasn't more than twenty minutes or so, and Pandermoan showed up with his weakened Horde. As he cast a raise the undead spell, I got up with the rest of the corpses. A few fake groans and he totally bought it.

While on his way to a small village just a few miles away I had to listen to him sing. He was awful. He made his minions applaud. Poor sap, no wonder he needed an undead audience. It reminded me of a traveling talent show that used to perform at Neverspring.

Next, it was jokes, Pandermoan told us awful, unfunny jokes. I pretended to laugh with the rest of the zombies as he beckoned but it was tough. Then finally he started telling tales of his childhood, like he wanted our pity or something, what a loser this guy was. I began daydreaming of slow acting poison and how he would twitch to it.

Finally, we entered the small village where he apparently had set up his home base. The enslaved villagers ran around scared, bowing and scraping at his every command because of their fear of his undead and his power. He led us all into the city square and started a long speech about how powerful he was and why girls liked him.

That's when he began singing again. That's also when I stepped up from behind and jammed my dagger Magurk through his skull. The song ended with "Magurk!" and the undead fell to the ground, free from the cleric's spell. The people of the village let out an almost deafening cheer and hoisted me up on their shoulders. If I didn't know any better, I'd swear the fallen zombies were smiling too.

Normally, I am not into this kind of festivities, but I had snagged my cloak back, and Swatfly's bow. Today was a day to celebrate indeed!

Entry 56

One yearly jubilee I tend to ignore is Fallfest. It's a magical time that folks come together to celebrate nature and brotherly love. Why can't the rest of the provinces give this thing a break? Some of us like to be a humbug and left to our vices.

There was this one Fallfest were I slipped into Shrively's Tavern for some quiet and a bowl of gruel, plus a bit of coin counting. The festivities in the streets were getting too loud and annoying to me. I sat there for a while listening to the complaints of other like-minded patrons; then I headed upstairs to the cheap room ol' Shrively saved for me.

As I laid in my bed with barely a few embers remaining in the fireplace, a ghostly apparition appeared before me. It's horribly burned face, and eyeless sockets jarred me at first, but then I realized who it had been. "It is I! The ghost of your guild coach, Purgis Uvloot!"

I regained my composure and sat up slowly, reaching for my dagger. "Put your blade down fool," it warned. "I'm here to introduce you to three ghosts who are here to visit you!"

"It looks like you didn't do so well in your solo challenge to Lavabreath, the ancient red dragon," I stated.

"That nogoodnik, Robbie the Thief, sold me a phony magic Vorpal Arrow of Instant Slaying!" he groaned. "So, basically, I shot at the dragon with a small twig of an oak tree!"

I didn't have the heart to tell him that I switched out the arrow when he wasn't looking. The arrow was way cool, and I couldn't resist it. "Where did you come from?" I asked.

"From a place hotter than that dragon's breath!" he exclaimed, while rattling his chains. "And you'll be there too, unless you change your ways!"

I rolled my eyes and sunk back into my blankets. "Goodnight, Purgis. Go scare somebody who cares."

Purgis laughed maniacally and waved his ghostly hands. That's when another apparition appeared. "Who is that?!" I said, sitting back up.

"I am Guffslump, the ghost of Fallfest past," it exclaimed. "I know how many times you've littered!"

Oh great, the ghost of a druid. It started ranting about the environment or something, so I threw my pillow at its face. It just sailed through it and hit the floor. "Get a real job, you vile smelling phantom!" I yelled.

Seeing that I was not phased, Purgis raised his spectral hands once more and summoned another." It was the ghost of an old man, in dark robes, with glittering stars all around. "I am Whifftoot, the slayer of the Blood Ogre, Keeper of Mysteries, Absolute Conqueror of the Dark Elfen under realm...."

"You sound like bad digestion to me," I said, waving my hand over my blanket.

"Listen to him, man. He is the ghost of Fallfest present!" Purgis pleaded.

"If he is a bad bit of digestion, he can present me with an antacid; I think I'll need it!" I replied, trying to remember if there were any strange tastes in the gruel that I ate.

All three ghosts frowned at me and started talking amongst themselves. "No, no, no," Purgis said, "Let's bring in the ghost of Fallfest Future."

With that said, the other ghosts reluctantly agreed. I pulled myself down under the covers, so only my eyes were peeking out. Purgis waved his hands once more, and the ghost of a giant bugbear appeared. "Grgoghne helufhn ehrou," it bellowed at me. "Trhoy hennyo pehvy!"

"I don't speak bugbear, you dolts!" I said to the ghosts, "Why don't you failures head back to wherever it is you came from!"

The apparitions all appeared angry, at this point and huddled together. After a quick mumbling, they all formed a line near my bed. "We've decided to take turns hurting you," Purgis said, with a big grin. "We were hoping you wouldn't have a revelation anyway."

As he finished his words, I pulled my magical Swatfly bow from under the blankets and notched an arrow. "A bow!?" Purgis laughed. "A bow is not going to kill a..."

That's when he noticed the Vorpal Arrow of Instant Slaying. The empty skull sockets grew large, and if it was at all possible, a frown formed on the skull face. "You thief!" Purgis screamed, as I let the arrow fly.

The arrow beheaded all four lined up ghosts in one shot. You see, your standard arrows can not hurt a ghost. But a magic bow and arrow can. As the ghostly crumpled bodies disappeared into an odorous mist, I went and picked up the broken arrow. It was a shame it could only be used once. Oh, well, it was worth it. Maybe Fallfest wasn't so bad, after all.

Entry 57

I have to admit, I enjoy the company of orcs, once in a while. Especially, when they are dead and I'm looting their bodies. They don't like being killed very much, though, so I guess I can understand. Dying is not a good way to live, that's why I try to avoid it.

There was this one time that I got into an argument with an angry orc captain about the ins' and outs' of my dagger blade. I won, of course, because it's hard to get the last word in when you're dead. Orcs love to argue about almost anything, well, at least I think they do. It's hard to tell when you don't speak a lick of orc. I don't believe they understand me either because no matter how hard I try to convince them that their gold coins should be mine, they just stare at me with glowing red eyes. Moments later, it all just ends up a bloody mess.

I think it's laziness on their part. If the doltish creatures would fix the squeaky boards in their huts, they wouldn't hear me at all, surround me, and try to take back all their treasure. I don't think they are civil either. After all, I took their valuables, fair and square.

I have generously given their stuff back a few times, especially after they've pummeled me senseless and chucked me into the woods. Orcs may be dumb, but they are by far, my favorite monsters to pester.

<hr>

€ntry 58

A local farmer, named John Himerschmidt from the Darkenbleak Province had come running into town one day, panicking over the fact that his love, "Jingal," was captured by a mad Illusionist, named Cobberfield. My party and I were just stocking up on dungeon raiding equipment at the local spelunk 'n' junk, so we immediately volunteered for the job.

Himerschmidt informed us that Cobberfield was heading towards the Temple of Temperamental Evil. Usually, I wouldn't hesitate to go into any dungeon, but I've never had good experiences at that place. Yet, there's always rumors of top notch treasure. Our big barbarian, YaMacha Derschingler, agreed immediately and I seconded the motion. The wizard, Saptoe, a fighter named Lewis, two twin ninja archers called Bok and Choy, and Healy the Cleric all agreed, so we set out immediately.

I had traveled with some of this group before, so I was pretty confident about entering the temple this time. Lewis was skeptical about me, as always. Talk about an unforgiving heart! All because I slipped a few coins out his pocket and he couldn't pay for a meal. It was only a week in the city's filthy jail; what's the problem?

On the way there, I always wondered what was past the first floor. I've been there so much that I could give it out as my address. The Temple of Temperamental Evil is known as the most dangerous place in the Unremembered Realms, but you'd think a person of my experience could make it down a level or two deeper.

When we reached the temple, we quickly dispatched a group of youngling lizard men. They were all pimply and spouting poetry when we confronted them. The first level of the temple was easy, since I had been there before. I disabled a poison dart trap in one room and found a secret door that got us some loot in another. We fought a few skeletons and few suicidal humans, who were dumb enough to challenge YaMacha. He beat one to death with his own arm. That was quite amusing!

It took awhile, and a few battles, but I found a secret switch that opened the door to a stairwell going down. There were lit torches, so I figured Cobberfield must have been here recently. When we crept our way down, we saw about fifteen guardsmen sitting in a large room playing cards and eating. At one of the tables, was Cobberfield himself. The minute he saw us, he yelled "Guards!" So much for the element of surprise!

Bok and Choy shot some arrows and instantly dropped about three guards before they even got up from their tables. YaMacha turned over one table, crushing two more. Saptoe ran in with lightning shooting from both hands, and Lewis fought simultaneously with two swords. Healy was doing some chant that made me feel a little stronger and faster, so I leapt on the biggest fighter I could find and slid onto his back. He tried to fight me off, but I had a built-in garrote wire that came from inside my bracers. He was lifeless in moments.

Cobberfield saw that we were a force to be reckoned with, so he shot a flame spell at YaMacha, and it burned him a bit, which only seemed to enrage him even more. The shaken illusionist opened a door at the far end of the room and began to run. Within a few seconds, we had finished off the guards and were running after him. We were almost on top of him, when I noticed him casting some hand spell. "Get ready," I thought to myself, but before I could blink, the floor went out from under me, and I began to fall. The floor was an illusion!

My entire party fell headlong into a 20-foot pit...with spikes at the bottom! Being slender and fast, I twisted myself just right and avoided the spikes, but I heard both my legs crunch as I hit bottom. Saptoe and Healy weren't so lucky. The wizard got a spike through the face, and the cleric had more holes than a voodoo doll. YaMacha had a spike through the leg. Lewis pulled his shoulder off one, but Bok and Choy seemed completely fine.

"Ha ha ha!" Cobberfield laughed. "Never chase an illusionist, fools!"

I tried to get up, but both my legs were broken. I'd probably be dead in an hour from internal bleeding. I never even made it to the third floor. What a disappointment! Cobberfield peered down at us over the edge "I am Cobberfield the Unstoppable!" he droned on, "Not even the mightiest of barbarians can stop...gack!"

Cobberfield stopped talking, because he received an arrow in each eye (I call this move the ole' 20/20). Bok and Choy were high-fiving each other, as Cobberfield's corpse fell over the edge and hit the spikes. We all were having a small chuckle through the pain, when we heard the water start to rush in. The trap was filling with water! The spikes lowered back into the floor, and we noticed a mechanical noise before the walls started moving in. "We'll float out the top!" Lewis yelled, as he began removing his armor. But some iron bars appeared over our heads and moved over us. We were trapped.

I appreciated the efforts of the craftsmen here; they thought of everything! YaMacha hobbled over to Cobberfield's dead body in panic mode. "This illusionist had to have something that can help us!" he yelled, with panic entering his voice. He found a small leather roll-up of vials. "Here's something! Does anyone know what these are?!"

"They could be poison, they could be magic," I said. The water was now past my elbows.

"Drink them and find out!" Lewis chimed. "You're going to die, anyway."

What a nice guy, I thought to myself, still bitter, I guess. But, he was right, what could it hurt? They all gathered around me as I gulped down all four vials. I didn't feel anything at first, and then I felt strength come back to my legs, lightness in my body, super strength, and then something happening with my eyes. I quickly rubbed them then a prismatic spray of colors erupted from them, hitting everyone around me.

Bok and Choy were affected by the green light and fell over fast

61

asleep into the water. YaMacha instantly turned to stone as the red light hit him. The blue light hit Healy, and he started getting up off the floor. Lewis got struck by the yellow light and got a big welcoming smile on his face. A purple light cut through the iron bars, leaving a gaping hole.

Feeling much better, and stronger, now that the eye lights stopped, I waited until the water was just deep enough and grabbed Bok and Choy and swam them up to the edge. As we all got out and caught our breath, I noticed a floor mat by a wall that read "Welcome to Cobberfield's." I searched till I found the secret door. The Illusionist wasn't as bright as we thought.

Inside his room, we found some magic items, which we gave to Healy and a health potion that Lewis gulped down quickly. I scored a large ruby, so we were quite pleased. That's when we noticed the small sewer rat, trapped in a cage on Cobberfield's desk. Written on a tag outside the cage was "Jingal."

Let's just say we didn't stick around the dungeon any longer. We had a new mission. I don't know if you've ever witnessed a farmer choke on a live rat before, but it's not pretty.

Entry 59

The Crimson Roof Guild wanted to expand, so they built a branch in the city of Amscray. Apparently, the yokels did not take kindly to having a bunch of thieves-in-training centered in their neighborhood. Since I happened to be around at the time, the leadership chose me to go and bring some peace to the tense situation.

I didn't mind going. The trip gave me something to do, and I liked Amscray. The taverns had tasty food and the jails were cleaner than your everyday lockup. I thought this was going to be a cushy assignment, indeed. Boy, was I wrong. When I showed up at the newly built guild, I noticed that it was constructed dead center in a community of druids.

The druids were holding all sorts of protests. Holding up signs, chanting, and singing songs about nature being upset with us.

When I first got there, they were in the middle of a hunger strike. In an attempt to smooth things over, I went out and introduced myself. Every day during lunchtime, I'd go out and listen to their rhetoric. I pretended to listen keenly, while eating my roast mutton or thick cut sandwiches. They kept giving me this look, like I was crazy or something, but after a few days, they hung on my every word. As warm grease dripped from my mouth onto my plate, they'd just stare longingly at the turkey leg I was biting.

During their chants, they'd hold up signs and scream "Thieves Go Home!" for hours on end. I thought it was awesome, because it gave me a chance to pick their pockets, while their hands were up and all that shouting covered up any noise I would make.

"Property is theft!" they'd yell, as they demanded we tear down our building. I agreed with them, so, at night, our students would go out and rob their homes. I thought this was kind of us to do, because materialism only hurts a true believer.

After a month, the head druid, Mayloxx, showed up at my door holding a white flag. He told me to take the land, because his small community was moving out to the woods, away from scum like us. I thanked him and wrote to the Dean of the Crimson Roof Guild about our success with the druids and how we reached an amicable agreement. He was jubilant that things worked out, because he tried to negotiate with these same druids in the past, but found that he could never stomach Mayloxx.

Entry 60

People always ask me why my right eye is so green. It's a common question because it has a slight glow, so it sticks out. Let me explain how I got it. It all started on a night just like any other, stabbing my way through a parade of monsters with my party, hoping to kill the guy or gal in charge. This particular time it turned out to be an alchemist.

After I had pushed through an archway and Magurk'd two goblin guards, I saw the alchemist in the final stages of his experiment. The evil scum had a lich's body lying on a table, and he was pouring the liquid into one of its eye sockets. I didn't see the goblin shaman pop out from behind him until it was too late. The green-skinned fool cast a magic missile at me, so when I did finally look up, it hit me in my eye, splattering it.

As I clutched my face, I saw my party fill the room and immediately butcher everyone in it. Logtoss the dwarf fighter came over and shook me to keep me conscious when I finally collapsed. "Are you going to live, thief?!" he growled as goblin blood dripped off his face. I was in some pain this time and could barely speak. Opening my left eye, I could barely make out our cleric, Fumblegums the Undentured doing something over the, yet to be raised, lich body. Its eyes were starting to glow green.

Fumblegums mumbled something indecipherable and stuck two fingers into one of its eye sockets and plucked one out. With a wink and a grin at Logtoss, he came at me. Before I could think Logtoss had me pinned while Fumblegums used Magurk to slice out the remainder of my right eye. He was chanting something through my screams as he jammed the lich's eye into the now empty socket.

I felt the eyeball meld itself into my socket. The pain began to subside after only a few moments, then all I could think of now was how heavy the dwarf was and how his armpit stank. The unwashed oaf reeked like a dead fish wrapped in ogre poo.

It had taken about a week before I gained complete vision back. I have no idea why that worked. But weeks later, I started noticing that, out of that eye, I could see at night, just like it was the day. I also noticed that I could see through a couple of layers of wood, if I concentrated hard enough. Handy for a rogue? You betcha! The nightmares and visions of the underworld that haunt me are well worth it!

Entry 61

I hate facebooks. No matter how small a town is, and no matter where I go in the provinces, there's always some local goody-two-shoes sheriff with a thick facebook lying on his desk and a drawing of me inside. It's never long before some cry baby points me out in a lineup and I have to plan some daring escape.

I also hate the fact that the law has been using druids to communicate with birds who witness my discrepancies. They are always twittering about this or tweeting about that. It made me kind of paranoid. Lately, I have to mark these birds, whenever I catch one. That way, I know which ones to avoid. I would normally just kill them, but a new law made tampering with their tweets a hangable offense!

Because of all of these things going against my freedom I have to stay linked in with my thieves guild brothers. They help me stay on top of new techniques used against people like me. Of course, when I want to know what the scoop is, I go to an old seer I call InstaGram. For the right amount of coin, the lovable granny uses a crystal ball to spy on my enemies. I see pictures that you wouldn't believe.

I used to sit with her for hours, as she would pour through all of the local posts looking for guild members who had been arrested. These outposts would pop up all over the realms; it didn't matter if you liked them or not. I had to quit visiting InstaGram, because going through the posts was using up all my free time. Plus, she started winking at me.

€ntry 62

While digging through my bag findings after not-so-tragic death of Cobberfield the Illusionist, I came across a shipment order. It was for a delivery of potions to be taken to a village of potential soldiers in exchange for their services. Apparently the whole crate of potions was labeled "Speed".

I love speed potions. You can get more done in a shorter period of time, that's for sure, and nobody would ever see you coming. Even if I could have only pinched a few of these I'd be happy. So I set off in the direction the map showed and wound my way around woods off the beaten path so I wouldn't be detected.

As the night fell I could see oranges and yellows lighting up the woods, it was a small village set ablaze. I didn't hear any screaming or running around so I approached cautiously. As the trees cleared I saw bodies, lot's of them. It was a massacre. Standing around the bodies and burning huts was a couple dozen large soldiers holding torches or moving in the direction of their wagon.

The strange this was, they were not moving very fast. In fact, they were moving incredibly slow. As I left the woods I walked up to one of the soldiers and saw what I just had began to suspect, Mansloths! Mansloths are fierce and cruel creatures, but very, very slow. Give them a potion of speed and they could whip an ogre single-handed.

They spotted me immediately and slowly started to point at me. Then they turned back towards their wagon. Some also started reaching in their pockets. I walked over to the wagon and found the mostly empty crate of speed potions. I pocketed about half a dozen before I sat down and started making journal notes about this.

After writing a couple of entries and a quick nap I woke up to see they were almost up to me now. Plus, the ones reaching into their pockets were still raising their potions up to their lips. I casually walked over and removed the potions and poured some poisons into their opened mouths.

I their slow changing expressions make me laugh unto this very day. I filled the wagon with a few wounded villagers, slew the rest of the mansloths, and headed off to a nearby cleric's house. What the hay, one good turn deserves another.

Entry 63

I once had a fight to the death with the loudest librarian in all the four realms. Her name was Abigail Sharmunn, and she would scream her head off at you when your books were late. Why the library would hire an actual Banshee is beyond me. These creatures could break a window with just a whisper.

So, there I was returning two books, "Proper Lockpicking by Needham Quick" and "How to Return Library Books Late by Portal

John." "This book must be a dud!" I explained to her, pointing to the book by Portal John.

"He didn't turn out to be the wise cleric he claimed," I explained. I got stuck paying the fine, plus I got a threat on my life by the undead hag.

"You're always late," she hissed. "I must claim your soul!"

So, it was a fight to the death. I thought this was kind of unfair, because she was already a creature of the living dead. But, being a gentleman and having an affinity to near death experiences, I agreed.

She flew through the desk at me and tried to rip out my throat with her ethereal claws; I deftly shifted to one side, while ducking. In her anger, she let out a wail that shattered the windows. Most of the customers were on the floor covering their ears and writhing in agony after that blast. One not-so-bright dwarf shushed her before she reached into his chest and devoured his soul.

While his body slumped to the floor, I grabbed the Portal John book and held it open on a page I had earmarked. Sharmunn looked at the page and screamed twice as loud, making almost all of us faint. Her whole ghostly form got sucked into the book in a phantasmal whirlwind. Then, the book fell to the floor and closed itself. "It worked!" I said, victoriously.

"Tip #22," I remarked to a fellow patron, who stood up and brushed broken bits of glass off his shoulders. "It's the page with all the clerical magic capture symbols for undead librarians."

I picked up the book and flipped a coin over the desk to the discombobulated librarian assistant. "You can red flag this book," I said. "I'm taking it the outhouse."

While not being known for being the most avid reader, I am known for "wiping" out my enemies! I guess they have me written down for harmin' Ms. Sharmunn.

Entry 64

Sometimes, a bit of a sense of humor can be deadly. Let me explain. I was sitting in the Loaf & Hammer Grill enjoying a meal when a portly wizard, named Fei Lo, walked over to the table where I was sitting and dropped a small wooden box in front of me.

Fei Lo, which means " the large man," was a well-known magic user; only the King of Rippenwind was more well known. "I'd love to be the King of Rippenwind someday," I thought to myself. Oh well, I sopped up the last bit of gravy from my plate with my bread and stuffed it into my mouth. Fei Lo shoved the box forward. I leaned in a little to inspect it. The box didn't seem like anything fancy to me.

"I need a rogue to deliver this to the High Wizard of Dragon-shelm," he said, while staring at me without blinking. "It's imperative, and I'll pay handsomely."

"How do you know I won't steal it?" I asked. "I may want to peek at it myself."

Fei Lo laughed, which shook his large belly. "Don't worry," he replied. "I'll help with that..."

The wizard waved his hands around, and a light circled the box and myself. Then, he turned to me with a grin. "Ta da!"

Nothing seemed to happen, so I just laughed. "Take your box and go home fool! I'm out of here!"

I didn't get far before noticing that the farther I got from the box, the more heated my body became. I was almost on fire before I turned around and ran back. "I don't think you want to be fired from this job," Fei Lo said, with a crooked grin. "All of your profit would go up in smoke!"

"Fine, I just won't deliver it at all then. I don't mind carrying your dumb box around." I told him, even though I was lying.

"Five days, Rogue," he said. "In five sunsets this box will explode, killing everyone within fifteen feet of it."

Fei Lo turned around and started to walk away. He stopped, turned his head slightly and said, "Dragonshelm is a three-day journey on foot. I wouldn't wait too long."

I wasn't too happy about the situation, but I've seen stranger things and there was a promise of coin. So, I got up, placed the small box in my pack, and headed out into the night air.

The journey was, indeed, a treacherous one. Through the dark mountains, across the rivers, which fed Two Snake Lake, and fighting through hordes of swamp life in Widowsmarsh. My dagger tasted so much blood on my journey that I thought it might need a diet more than Fei Lo. But, alas, who am I kidding? I wouldn't deny Magurk the sweet taste of Fei Lo's blood, if I got the chance.

After the three-and-a-half-day journey, I came to Purgewater in the Province of Dragonshelm. I approached the high wizard's Manor and only had to show the box to be let in. His pad was an opulent estate loaded up with all sorts of goodies that I wouldn't mind getting my hands on. His butler, an old human, named Mankey, was apparently suffering from some horrid skin disease. He led me up a long, winding staircase up into the high wizard's office.

The office was a what's what of your classic wizard fare. Potions, books, and magical items. The old man even had a pile of board games. "My boss never lets me win," Mankey whispered. "He's a horrible cheat!"

Mankey introduced me to the high wizard, who was at his desk reading a children's joke book and giggling to himself. "So, you are the famous delivery boy," he chirped. "Hand it to me, Gwai Lo."

Gwai Lo is a nickname I got in my youth; it means "ghost man." I pulled the box from my pack and handed it to him. He signaled to Mankey the Butler and pulled out a small coin sack and set it in front of me. The wizard slowly opened the box and pulled out a small scroll. As he unrolled it, a giant grin grew on his face. He quickly pulled out a small scroll of his own and started writing. He placed the scroll back into the box and waved his hand over it.

"What is going on?" I asked, my blood starting to boil, as I realized this little game wasn't over.

"Same rules," he said, smirking, as he picked his joke book back up. "Now scram, before I curse you with a skin rash!"

Mankey hurried me out the door, and with a sad look, closed the doors behind me. "Oh well," I thought to myself. "I guess I'll buy myself a little dinner." I opened the coin sack to see there were only nine gold coins and an old button.

Let's just say I wasn't too pleased about this and started dreaming of ways I could make the lives of these two a lot shorter. As of that moment, there was nothing I could do so I continued the deliveries, the life-threatening battles, and the cross realm treks. On the fifth delivery, the nightmare finally came to an end when the high wizard opened the last scroll and nearly fell over out of his chair laughing. That's when I finally got a peek.

In a relatively simple script, it read, "Orange you glad I'm not a banana?"

A knock-knock joke. I risked life and limb and got a pittance of a reward for a knock-knock joke! Now that I was free, I decided to visit Fei Lo and tell him one last knock-knock joke of my own. I can still remember his last words. "Assassinating who?"

Entry 65

I know it seems like I hate every festival in the Unremembered Realms, but there is one that I hate most of all...the Ashberry Festival. Once a year, the Ashberry trees sprout their little black berries, and people use them for food, wizards use them for spells, and I use them as bait when hunting birds.

I can understand why some people like to make a big deal out of it, but some people get more excited than others, and Ashberry Festival is no exception. I was traveling through the Province of Dragonshelm for a couple of weeks, and I holed myself up in the town of Humderum at the Fowl Odor Tavern. The tavern was famous for roasting the best birds, especially during Ashberry Festival time, when birds would migrate there.

I had just laid down to go to sleep, when I heard "bong, bong, bong, tap, tap, bong" over and over again, in some off-rhythmic beat. Then, it would stop. As soon as I dozed out, "bong, bong, bong" again. I'd had enough. The sound was coming from the room next to mine, so I marched over and pounded on the door.

The bonging stopped, and I heard shuffling. Within moments, the door opened. Standing there with an Ashberry wreath circling his head, was a druid. Further into the room, was a whole group of druids, dressed the same way. They were all sitting in a circle and playing the bongos. "What's the problem constable...we're cool," he stated.

"I'm not a constable, just your neighbor, and I am trying to sleep," I said. "Could you please keep it down?!"

"Far out man, we can dig it," he smiled, while looking me over. "What are you man, an assassin or something?"

"Trust me," I answered, "you don't want to know."

"That's cool, man. We're hip. Don't want to drag down your mystery vibes," he said, while holding up two fingers in a "V" shape. "We're not killers; we like nature and stuff...we're into vegetable rights and peace."

I hate Ashberry Festival. It always gets ruined by these yahoos. If I had my way, they would all be in wood stocks by now. I would spend all my gold coins for the biggest and ripest tomatoes and let them have it.

"Would you care if I joined you?" I asked.

"That's so groovy," he replied. "C'mon in mystery dude..."

"I hope you don't mind if I bring my food in here," I replied.

"Que sera, sera," he said, rejoining his circle. "We accept all sorts; this is a no judgment zone."

I quickly left and came back holding a live goose. The druids all stopped playing and looked at me. "That's a strange pet," the chief druid said observing the situation.

"This is not a pet," I replied. "It's my dinner!"

With that said, I whipped out Magurk and started in on my bird. The blood sprayed the faces of the druids, as well as their bongo's. As they screamed and ran out of the room, I just stood there and enjoyed the quiet. I wasn't hungry; I had only gotten it to scare the druids. I took the bloodied bird and stuffed it into one of the druids travel packs.

When I got back to my room, I laid back down and started to snooze again. The druids eventually came back, but the only noise was their crying, which I found comforting, and drifted into sleep.

Entry 66
You can never be friendly to pirates. One minute, you're chatting

with them about how much gold you think they might have on their ship and the next minute you're captured, whilst trying to steal it. The brig isn't all that bad, though, the rats have the softest mange and can be quite tasty, if you're desperate.

One time, on a ship called The Dragon Bottom, they didn't even bother to tie me up. So, I picked the lock on the cage door and kindly stabbed the sleeping guard. I snuck out and shadow-walked to the nearest cannon room, where I proceeded to aim it at the floor. It's amazing how fast a ship can sink. I felt kind of bad after that, mostly because of all the water in my lungs.

I did manage to make it to the surface and grab some floating debris. The captain, an overweight fellow named PlankTon, was such a nice guy. I'll never forget his last words, as I watched him drown, "I'll come back from the dead with my crew and take care of you!"

I'm still flattered that someone would want to take care of me, even though I killed their entire crew. Little did I know, that someday I would meet all them again, on a ghost version of the same ship! But, that's a story for another time.

<hr>

Entry 67

Shuffleball has been the number one sport in the Unremembered Realms for as long as I can remember. Every province provides a team of ten zombies. The teams are made up of zombies who haven't rotted away enough to be unable to move. They are set loose on the field with the ball sitting between both teams. The specially made ball is a brain wrapped in a magical shell. Whichever team makes it to the designated area with the brain wins a point.

Everyone has their favorite, but mine happens to be the Darkenbleak Shufflers. Not only do I like the Shufflers get-up-and-go, but their coach is a real spirit, literally. Last year they seemed dead in the water, but that was because it rained.

Things can get pretty intense at these games. I've bitten off quite a few fingernails. You just have to remember to check and see if it's you biting your nails and not some member of the team. Better that than sitting on the edge of your seat, though. I've seen fans fall over the barrier wall in their excitement. I've seen the same fans appearing as players the following week. The other downside to being a fan, is following your favorite players. Not only are they rotten from the get-go, but it's sad to watch them fall apart over time.

Entry 68

One day, I was waiting outside the local jail around the sleazier side of the city of Thudbunker. My associate Aggression, the Rogue, had been locked up and probably tortured for a while, so I came there to pay off an official and save him from the gallows. Why? Because he knows the secret switch codes on a nearby treasure cave that a wizard thought was totally hidden.

Earlier that week Aggression and I had been rescuing some gold from a few houses in the area when he got pinched. Lucky for him, as I got away, I snatched up the collected loot that he dropped; which, had been easy to do, since I had already bribed a corrupt constable to find us and snag him. You see, in this situation, everyone was a winner!

Surprisingly, they just let him go without me paying, so I treated him to lunch at the Wink & Gobble; a more upscale tavern on the north side of Thudbunker. I ordered him a hot bowl of stew from the kitchen. "I'll never forget what you've done," he said to me, as he chewed his stew slowly.

It must have been hard to eat with his face swollen up from all the jailhouse beatings. But, I did appreciate his thankful spirit. "Lunch is on me," I said, with a grin. "It's the least I can do."

"Where is my share of the loot?" he asked.

"Where are the switch codes for the cave?" I replied, casually.

"I'll have them soon, fool!" came a voice from behind me. "Aggression and I have a deal now-50/50."

The corrupt constable approached me from behind. "It's the torture cell for you, rogue!"

His men grabbed me by the arms and lifted me from my chair.

"You can't trust anyone nowadays!" I yelled at Aggression, as they drug me away. If he was smiling, I couldn't tell.

I couldn't stop chuckling to myself while being locked up. I knew the constable and his little band of cheats would probably be dead by now and I also knew the backstabber, Aggression, would be here any minute with my half of the treasure. The slow acting poison I slipped in his stew should have kicked in by now. "Pssst!" I heard, along with some coughs from outside the jail window. I held up the antidote, and he held up a large sack of gold. We both smiled.

Entry 69

While I was hanging around the shopping district of Amscray, I bumped into a large red-haired fighter wearing a kilt. I figured he must be clumsy, because he accidently dropped his coin purse into my hand. I know this, because when I ran off to hide, there it was. I peeked around inside to find about thirty-five gold and a few coppers. Also inside, was a snazzy looking ring and a note to Kiltus Slamhammer from some person, named Striver. It was hard to read the sloppy handwriting.

Outside of the slip of paper, it read "Top Secret," but on the inside, it contained only these six mysterious words: One ring to rule the mall. "This ought to get me a few coins down at the Token Exchange Pawn Shop," I thought to myself.

I hurried through the busy crowd until I found the shop. There was a grubby little halfling there who loved shiny things. He was keen to see the ring, for some reason. The bug-eyed halfling kept saying the ring was very precious. What a fool. I wrangled two hundred gold out of him, before slipping back out into the street.

As I walked out, I was nearly knocked over by the red-haired fighter and a small crew pushing their way into the Token Exchange. I didn't want to stick around after hearing a bunch of yelling and smashing, so I made haste to hide in a nearby orange drink shop.

I never understood why Kiltus would care about a ring that

would give him the ability to "Rule the mall." Hmmm...I wonder if
I read that wrong...

Entry 70

For once, I had a few extra coin, so I decided to do a bit of shopping at the Port of SeaBay. It's an auction port off the coast of the
Province of Darkmist. The best way to get there is to sail, because
of the hordes of undead, legions of orcs, and flesh-eating trolls
that live in the land surrounding it.

The creatures thrive in this area, so the Wizards of the Coastline
have built up a magical firewall to keep out most of them. Yeah,
they can stop the trolls, but the hackers (i.e. orc shaman with fire
resistant weapons) manage to get through once in a while and dis-
rupt their business.

The best way to shop is to go overseas. The problem is that you
have to sail through The Baremoon Triangle, which is legendary
for making ships disappear. I hired a sailor with a small tourist
boat-just a local clown and his crew of flunkies. They were desperate for coin, so I got a decent price. We left Gaspenfall out of Port
Laudervale and sailed through the mostly sunny weather.

The minute we crossed into the Baremoon Triangle, a huge storm
appeared and tossed us around like a spitball in a classroom of
hooligans. Flunky spotted a lighthouse and we headed straight for
it. One of his four crewmen started to panic when it looked like we
were too weighted down. He pointed at me and started ranting on
about a curse or something. The rest of the crew were too busy
keeping the boat above water, so it was up to me to calm him
down.

Let's just say he got a little overboard with his thinking. Things
seemed to go better after that, now that the "curse" was removed.
Not only that, but the boat was that much lighter, so we managed
to guide it along the shoreline.

It was storming pretty badly, so we kept going in the direction of
the lighthouse. We managed to get ashore and take a few moments
to catch our breath. On the way to the lighthouse, we spotted three

other small boats with orcish scribblings all over them.

We smashed holes into their sides just in case there was trouble. Flunky was all panicking about the orcs, but I reassured him everything would be okay...unless they killed us. The storm was picking up, so we ran the rest of the way to the bottom of the spiral stairs that wrapped around the outside of the lighthouse. The crew almost ran off when they saw the two dead human soldiers at the bottom step. "This is a bad omen!" Flunky shouted. "I wish our top fighter hadn't gone overboard!"

"We don't have time for wishes," I shouted, through the rain. "We've got to get to the top!"

About halfway up, Flunky turned to me and shouted, "I think we're going to make it!"

That's when a flaming barrel of oil appeared from around the corner and swept him over the side. The crew and I looked over the edge just in time to see the explosion at the bottom. "He might be okay," I reassured them. "It is raining pretty hard."

"If only our cleric hadn't gone overboard!" one of the crewmen cried aloud. "He could have healed him!"

"I thought it was the fighter that went overboard?" I asked.

"He had many skills," he replied. "He was just superstitious, that's all."

"Things will be fine. Leave this to me..." I told him, as a crossbow bolt went through his red tunic, straight into his heart.

As he fell over the side, I did a backflip and threw a couple of throwing knives at the heat source that I could see through my Lich eye. There was a mild screech, then whatever it was fell over. The two remaining crewmen and I ran over and carefully flipped over the body. It was an orc crossbowman. Within moments, we were bounding up the steps and fighting two orc guardsmen who were standing by the lighthouse door.

Orcs don't know much, as far as fighting techniques, just smash and kill, so I was able to stab one to death fairly quickly. The other one was just wiping a crewman's brain off his war hammer, when I ran and slid between his legs holding up Magurk as I went. He danced around a bit before falling over a couple of oil barrels, which also fell over and started pouring down the steps.

The remaining crewman stood up on the steps and tore off his red tunic, revealing large muscles. "I don't know about you," he screamed, angrily "but I can hear a group of these thugs coming up the steps and I'm not going to die today!"

He reached down and soaked his tunic with oil. "Got a flame I can borrow?" he asked, as he peered down at the oil covered steps and the group of warrior orcs coming up them.

Just as he finished that question, a flaming arrow went through his chest, in the back, and out the front. The flame was still going and lit the tunic he was holding on fire. The poor guy fell face first into the oil on the stairs and immediately lit the entire staircase on fire, igniting all of the oncoming orcs.

I didn't have time to stay and watch them leap off the side, so I used my Blending Cloak to dodge the next few arrows. I sprinted and jumped through the window tackling the last remaining orc who was in the lighthouse tower. He was quite the bleeder! It's a good thing my cloak was already soaked and a little stain resistant. The cleaning bills on magic cloaks are outrageous.

Apparently, I had gotten rid of him just in time, because off in the horizon, sailing towards the lighthouse, was a fleet of orc warships. I don't know what these orcs had planned, but I spent the rest of the evening steering their warships toward the rocks, using the lighthouse beacon. Once that was over, I had a quick peek around. It turned out that the orc had a few coins and even a couple of nice magic arrows!

I eventually found the lighthouse keeper's journal. He had been into some shady deals with the orcs and been taking some coin from them for some upcoming invasion on SeaBay.

After collecting the loot off the bodies the next morning, I headed back to the shoreline to find the boat we left. Can you guess who was standing by it at the beach? The fighter/cleric crewman! What a great bit of luck!

"Sorry I called you cursed," he said, as I approached. "I guess I'm just an old nervous sea dog; in my panic, I even slipped overboard!"

"That's okay," I replied. "I do have a tendency to make people nervous."

After plundering the dead orcs, we sailed over to SeaBay and loaded up on the latest gear. I even opened a line of credit with their new BayPal system, which didn't work out too well for them, in the long run. I am a thief, after all.

Entry 71

One night, I had snuck over the gated wall that protected the biggest house in Neverspring. I was attempting to quietly ransack the mansion of the incredibly corrupt Mayor Cofferdip. He was not well liked, so I didn't feel too bad helping myself to a few his ill-gotten gains.

I had heard through the grapevine he was hosting a meeting with some fellow bigwigs, so I figured he would be distracted. I wandered down some of the polished hallways, taking whatever small items I could pocket. I blended with the shadows whenever an armed guard would appear.

It didn't take long before I heard laughing from behind a nicely carved wooden door, so I crept up and put my ear to it. What I began to overhear, was a secret cabal to control businesses throughout the realm and maximize profits for this group of men and their semi-human friends. As I loaded my sack with the valuable from their coats and cloaks, I thought about how crooked these people were. It was in moments like these that I lost all hope in humanity.

I missed my last adventuring party, but on a stealth robbery like this, I needed to work alone, rather than have some fumbling barbarian blasting his way down the hallway. I just wanted to get in quickly and leave just the same. At the moment when I turned around to leave, I bumped into a stand. The vase sitting on top of it made a loud crashing noise as it hit the floor, sending pieces tinkling down the hardwood floor. Within seconds I was surrounded by armed security and most of the guests from the meeting. I gave a little smile and held up my hands in surrender to the large group of frowning faces.

I was hauled into the meeting room, tied up in a chair, and

placed into the middle of a circle of tables. A cute blonde waitress hand fed me an Hors d'oeuvre, as I listened patiently, while the group tried to figure out how to kill me and dispose of my body. I don't know what they agreed upon, because I quit listening after awhile. All I could think about was some of the nice jewelry they were wearing. Then, they all started to applaud and cheer. The Mayor, an older chap with a neatly trimmed beard, strolled up to me and pulled out a jewel encrusted broad ax with a blue flame that swirled around the blade.

"That's fantastic!" I said, admiring the axe. "It must be worth a fortune!"

"You will be cut in half and fed to the swine, " he said, nonchalantly while firming his grip and getting ready to swing.

"Make sure you get my good side," I said while raising one of my Speed Boots in between his legs. "Ohhh!!' he cried out. So did the others that were watching.

Just as that happened, a guard came flying through the door...literally. His body caved the door in half and his corpse hit the shag carpet with a thud and a tumble. There, standing in the hallway, was a huge barbarian with his eyes bugging out, blonde hair flowing, and his battle cry emanating from his lips! The room erupted in chaos as YaMacha Derschingler, followed by Bok and Choy the ninja archers, and Healy the cleric ran around the room killing everyone in sight. Mayor Cofferdip tried to stand up, but the waitress jumped in front of me, yelled out some words, and froze him inside a block of ice.

YaMacha ran around the room cleaving through the remaining cabal members, "Excuse me, pardon me," he yelled. After breaking his ax blade on the skull of a thick-headed dwarf, he quickly picked up the dwarf and used his corpse to beat to death the remaining guests. Barbarians are such nice fellows.

"I thought you were dead?" I asked YaMacha, as I tried to untie myself from the chair.

"I would have been, no thanks to you, rogue." he said slowly turning to me, blood splatters dripping from all over him.

"While you ran off to spend your gold," Bok chimed in, "we used our portion to hire this new wizard, named Aloonda."

The waitressing wizard gave me a slight bow and a wink. "I went back into the Temple of Temperamental Evil with them and reversed the stone spell that was on YaMacha," she said.

"I spent mine on good times and a new treasure map from Robbie the Thief," I explained as I finally got myself loose.

"You're spending days are over rogue!" YaMacha said as he started walking toward me. "You are a traitor!"

Not wanting to be on the bad side of this lunatic I ran over to the mayor, who was following me with his eyes from inside the ice block and aggressively ripped the magic axe from him. I say ripped, literally, because his frozen arm came off with it! The mayor's eyes got really big. He must've felt shocked that I took his prize axe.

"I came here to find this beautiful weapon, YaMacha." I lied. "I was going to come back, but I didn't want to come empty-handed!"

Healy and Choy were making gagging motions with their fingers in their mouths, but apparently, YaMacha was touched. He shook the mayor's arm off onto the floor and held up the ax. "This feels good!" he exclaimed, before shouting, "All is forgiven!"

The party was once again reunited, and I felt pretty good about it. We even shared an elegant meal by picking up the non-bloodied food off the floor. Most of the furniture got smashed, so I ended up using one of the fatter dead guys as a chair, while I ate.

The mayor looked on from his frozen prison, while we went over the new treasure map I had mentioned. We took off on the next quest and let the mayor slowly unthaw. He didn't seem like too much of a threat, now that he was unarmed.

Entry 72

Shamptown has a parade they call the Trail of Jeers. They gather up all the prisoners from the jails and march them to the gallows for a swinging party! It's a great celebration, if you're not one of the chained captives. Believe me, I've seen it from both sides.

Some of the mocking can be hurtful to most, but I get a kick out of a good solid taunt. I get some of my best lines from all the verbal abuse. When I'm not one of the prisoners, I'm busy writing down some of these great one-liners.

Thanks to my Hat of Disguising, I never end up at the rope. I just put it on and the jailers panic, as I walk off. "Where'd he go?", "Have you seen a guy with one green eye?", and "You smell just like him!" are some of the things I hear as I'm making my getaway. The residents of Shamptown don't pay too much attention, though; they just want to see a few villains take the short drop. The audience would get so distracted by this event, that I could pick a few pockets, without being detected. Shamptown townsfolk come up with the best taunts and jeers; I swear it's comedy gold!

I was marching the Trail of Jeers one day, and noticed a fat dwarf, named Noneck. He had been caught stealing multiple times, and each time they tried to hang him, the noose would just slide away because his neck was larger than his head! The little worm got off the hook every time.

This event would not be worth remembering, had not I noticed something strange occurring in my dungeon crawls. I'd be taunting out with my "A" material, and it wouldn't even phase the creatures or evil people that I'd fight. "Heard it!" They'd cry out, while I was trying to stab them. "It was funnier the first time!"

"Noneck!" I'd say, through clenched teeth.

The little dwarf was using the best taunts before I got the chance. To a professional taunter like me, this is devastating. He was even using some of my taunts that I'd been developing for months. It was evident that he was a hack and loved to steal material from others. Where's the honor in that?!

Entry 73

A highlight in the town of Brokenpoor is a fantastic Dry Cleaner, named Pumice. He was a high-ranking wizard who was a germophobe. I guess he got tired of fighting monsters and decided that bacteria was a much bigger threat.

He is quite a pleasant fellow and his prices just can't be beaten.

For example, I brought in a leather chest piece that a zombie was trying to bite through when it sneezed. The mucous was so thick that it hardly dripped. Pumice didn't even flinch. He ran it into the back room and voila! Ten minutes later he was back with the piece looking good as new.

One day, I brought in my Speed Boots, because they had smelled bad from crossing a farm field. Whatever I had stepped in was fresh, because the odor was burning my eyes. When I took them into Pumice's shop, he twiddled his fingers with delight, then smiled as he licked his lips. The old wizard seemed to love a challenge. With a tip of my hat and a coin changing hands, I turned toward the door. I was planning to go to the local tavern for a meal and to study the plans of a nearby fortress that some orcs were building.

"He licks the clothes clean," a child's voice spoke out of nowhere.

It caught me off guard, but then I looked down and saw a little girl holding a stuffed owlbear doll. "What did you say?" I asked.

"I said he licks the clothes clean," she continued. "One of Mr. Grumpywho's button eyes fell out when he cleaned him, so I snuck back when he was seeing another customer. He didn't know I was there, so I watched him lick clean all the dirty laundry."

I have to admit; I was a little surprised at this. "Are you sure?" I asked in disbelief.

"Oh yeah, he seemed to enjoy the grossest stuff," she giggled, while walking past me and out the door.

I had heard of Bogwizards, but I never thought I would meet one. Legend had it that they gained power and knowledge through dirt, grime, and slime. They could track a man by licking his footprint. They could even discover your deepest secrets by sucking on your used handkerchief.

Within moments, I jumped over the counter and ran into the backroom. Behind the curtain, Pumice was sitting in an overstuffed brown chair, tongue buried deep into my left boot. It looked like the wizard was in some kind of euphoric state. When I pulled my boot from his hand, he snapped out of it with a startled yelp.

"So, you know my secret!" he said slowly, rising from his chair.

"And you know mine," I said, reaching in my cloak.

"This doesn't have to get ugly..." he stated, cracking his knuckles.

" I hope not," I replied. "I don't want to lose my discount."

"Wait, what?!" he said, shaking his head. "You, you don't want to kill me?!"

"Not really, I don't care if you lick boots, cloaks, or snot rags," I said, "Your prices can't be beaten, and you do an excellent job!"

Pumice just smiled and picked up my other boot, "So you don't mind if I finish?"

"Not at all. I just wanted to see if you could hurry up with the boots," I remarked. "I need to raid an orc fortress tomorrow!"

For years, I have kept the old man's secret, and you, dear reader, if you want a good price on dry cleaning, must keep your mouth closed as well.

Entry 74

The Unremembered Realms are made up of four realms; each one has its king. So, the character of the current king usually reflects what is happening in their realm at that present time. Each realm is divided up into three provinces; which, are led by elected governors. Each one of these governor's success depends on whether they can balance the king's laws with the will of the people who voted them in.

From that point, each realm has a bunch of cities; big and small. Most of them have a mayor, or even just some kind of sheriff, if the town is small enough. The point of all this explanation is that if you're going to run a scam that gets the attention of all these individuals, then you, sir or madam, are one smart cookie.

One of the reasons I got the nickname "Gwai Lo" or "Ghost Man," was because of my ability to cause a stir, then disappear. I've been called many other names, but I don't want to list them in case women or children are reading my journal. One of my favorite bits was to run into a small village after a nasty dungeon fight, because I was rough looking after a few encounters. I'd shout "They're coming! They're coming! Run!"

Usually, the townsfolk would run off to the woods as fast as they could, leaving most of their goods behind. This reaction would give me a chance to catch up on some shopping. Mind you, I do have a heart; I'd only take a little gold from each. Plus I wouldn't take all the food, just my unfair share. I always loved it when someone left their hotpot on the fire. Homemade cooking is not something you get every day in my line of work. Living life on the road means you get sick of fast food, especially when it's so hard to catch.

Little did I know, that my scam was causing quite a stir in the realms. From kings, all the way down to the sheriffs, I was getting something of a reputation. Eventually, all the leaders agreed to assemble a special task force to hunt me down. What a flattering gesture!

They had calculated, through my travel patterns, that my next appearance would be at the Hamlet of Miftenmad, just south of the Tanglewood Forest in the Realm of Farlong. They were right on the button. Earlier that day, I had barely survived a job trying to recover a magic dog whistle from a group of hill giants who'd been using it to summon and chain demon dogs to raid the southeast portion of the Hoktu Mountains.

I was beaten up, so I made a direct path to Miftenmad. As I ran in shouting "They're coming!" about fifty royal guardsmen came out of the huts in the village and surrounded me. These were large, heavily armored men who bore the seals of all the Unremembered Realms. "We don't see any threat, Gwai Lo!" one said as he stepped up before me.

"Who?" I asked, pretending to be unaware of the situation.

He signaled one of his men who walked up and unrolled a scroll in front of me. It was my face, or at least an uncannily accurate drawing of it. "Never seen him before," I lied.

The giant warrior poked his metal-gloved finger into my chest and said, "If nothing shows up in the next five minutes...you're going to wish they had!"

The soldiers were all smiling, at this point, and looking eager to use their weaponry. "I don't think they'd waste time with you cowards anyway," I remarked. As the leader started pummeling me, along with a few of his other men, I had time to slip the chain that held the whistle off my neck. I blew into it a few times and thrashed around, trying to avoid most of the blows. I grabbed onto the leader, but he just threw me back down.

Within moments, the trees by the hamlet split open, and about half a dozen hill giants emerged, along with their gigantic demon dogs. The guards quit hitting me and whipped around with their weapons drawn. "Give us our whistle!" The largest giant said, "or we will grind your bones for breakfast!"

Before the leader of the soldiers could respond, I pointed at him. "There it is, around his neck!" I yelled.

Shocked, the leader looked down at his chest and slowly realized what I had done, while they were happily beating me. "I'm going to get you for this, ghost man!"

With that said, the angry soldier, along with his men, ran full charge into the giants and their dogs. As I made a run for the woods, I saw the scroll with my face on it lying on the ground. I snagged it up and hid in a hut, while I made a few changes to the drawing. As I ran back and dropped off the scroll, I noticed that the giants were dragging their victims off into the woods.

A few months later, I had heard through the grapevine that the kings of the realms were celebrating the capture of "The Ghost Man." I hope my associate Robbie the Thief didn't mind my little prank too much. Altering the drawing was easy, plus it even gave him some of my rugged good looks.

Entry 75

One time, I was lost somewhere in Darkmist with an Illusionist named Towfungus. We had been with a larger party who had fought a lich in its underground lair below a graveyard. Towfungus and I both agreed it was time to leave, after watching it drink the souls of our friends.

As we worked our way through the ravine of some nearby hills, we spotted a cave we could sleep in overnight. He was a bit skeptical of the cave, so I scouted ahead using my magical Blending

Cloak. I was only about twenty-five feet into the cave when I heard the sound of a woman crying. I only took a few steps, before I felt the tip of some weapon at my back.

I put my arms up, slowly, and obeyed my captor's directions. "Go on little lamb, move along."

Whatever it was, marched me into a room full of all sorts of monsters, all of which were incredibly obese. The crying of the woman stopped, as all attention was now on me. "Hello," I waved a little, with a fake smile.

The woman I heard crying wasn't a female as you'd think. She was a Drider; which, is half a dark elf and half a spider. She was wiping off her tears and looking at me like I was dinner. "What are you doing here, dumpling!" she spat at me. "Can't you see I'm trying to lose weight!"

The other monsters all shook their heads in agreement. Apparently, this was a self-help group for creatures who were trying to drop a little weight. A greasy haired ogre that was sitting next to her patted one of her legs. "There, there, Girtha, remember our pledge," he reminded her. "Portion control is the goal!"

"Thank you, Moger," she replied. "I will resist this temptation. What say the rest of you?"

An overly plump minotaur sneered at me. "Looks wiry anyway."

But, then, a very flabbulent orc in a loin cloth came over and started sniffing me. "I wouldn't mind a snack," the creature admitted loudly with a bit of drool dripping from its mouth. "I bet this thief's liver is extra moist!"

"I agree," said the voice of the guard standing behind me. "Let's eat him raw!"

I looked behind me to see a chubby little kobold holding a sharp stick. How embarrassing, I thought to myself. The others started shrugging their shoulders and I could tell things weren't looking too good for me. "Listen, Girtha," I spoke up. "Do you have any children?"

She started sobbing, "No! I always eat my mate before anything happens," she sobbed. "I'm so ashamed.

Moger the Ogre stood up and started to give her a hug. "Me too!" he cried.

During the hug, I noticed she started tasting Moger's shoulder... and he hers. That's when it happened. The flabby orc, kobold, and I were nearly knocked over by a lich that came barreling into the cave. "I did it again!" it cried, while standing before the fire in the middle of the room. "I ate more souls!"

"Let it out, Charlie," Moger said, with a touch of blood running down his shoulder. "We're here for you."

Through hiccupping tears, the lich told his story of sucking the souls out of my party and eating them all at once. "I didn't even save one for dessert!" he sobbed.

"Things could be worse," the orc chimed in. "At least you won't be hungry for a while!"

This advice made the Lich cry more, "No, no, no..." it moaned. "I picked up a snack by the door! It doesn't seem like my thirst will ever be quenched!"

Oh well, I thought, there goes the illusionist. I'll probably run faster without Towfungus anyway. Then, I had an idea while listening to the pathetic whinings of these creatures. I slowly unsheathed Magurk and started to slice my hand. When the orc wasn't looking, I let my blood drip onto his leg. It wasn't long before the chubby little kobold caught the scent and did a big bite on the orc's leg.

"Aaahh!!" it screamed in pain. "Trying to eat me eh?! I'll eat you, myself!"

With that said, all the creatures started trying to eat each other as if in some bizarre buffet. I slipped out of the cave and back over the hill. In my haste, I nearly tripped over Towfungus's depleted corpse in my haste. It was that day I learned that I could turn "self help" into "help yourself" with just a wave of my hand!

Entry 76

It is said that I may have been the cause behind the near-destruction of the race of dworc's that existed in all four of the realms. What are dworcs? Let me explain. Many moons ago, on the Island of Hemridge, off the northwest coast of Farlong, lived a small family of orc's, known only as the Hemfield's. They made their living by raiding farms on the mainland. Also on the island, was a family of dwarves who were, unsuccessfully, mining the hills of Hemridge. They were known as the MacRoy's.

As legend has it, the Hemfields and MacRoy families fought for generations, until two of their younglings fell in love and got married. This wedding gave way to the beginning of a new race of beings, called dworcs, half-dwarf, and half-orc. Not only that, but the two families joined forces, and in honor of the new peace treaty, they changed their family's names to the Hemroys. From that time forward, they were a real pain in the behind for everyone in the surrounding islands.

My story began when I was at the Scuttlebutt Tavern, picking at my usual plate of Mystery Salad. After eating, I felt a bit nauseous, so I slipped into the tavern's latrine. I found what I thought was an empty stall and nearly sat on a Hemroy! He was a small, ugly thing, and smelled like he'd been in here awhile. "I saw what you ate," he stated, as I flew out of the stall. "So, I knew you'd be in here shortly."

"I came in here to do some business," I confessed, "Not to listen to yours!"

"Then you mustn't be the armor dealer I was supposed to meet?" he asked, keeping his voice low.

I had no idea what he was talking about, but I decided to play along. "Oh, the armor deal! That's me," I lied. "Anything for a price!"

The little dworc smiled, showing off spacious gaps between his teeth. He then started to prattle on about how on the neighboring island of Hickleweiss, a new training camp of soldiers training with lances had recently sprung up. I guess their mission was to kill all the dragons in the four realms. The only problem with their work happened while trying to build their training facility. They cut some stones from the local hillsides and discovered some gold.

This discovery was too much for the dworcs to handle. They had been mining on the wrong island for years. They were hankering for a feud like in the old days, so they started plotting a raid on Hickleweiss. The only problem, was the Hemroy clan knew the soldiers would kill them all with their superior modern weaponry. "The lances are very deadly," he stated. "We need some top notch shields if we're going to stand a chance!"

"You leave that to me," I assured him. "I know just what to do."

It just so happened that Robbie the Thief was in town and I knew he had some connections with this building supply group located on the nearby island of Taiwan. So after the dworc paid me half down, I met with Robbie and he met with this supplier who agreed to make the shield's for a quarter of the down payment from the ugly little imp! I could hardly sit down over this Hemroy deal, so I flipped Robbie a few coins for his trouble and hung out in town for a month, while I waited for the order of shields to come in from the island of Taiwan.

As per the agreement, the boxed up order of one hundred shields showed up to the shipyard, right on time. I chartered a local ship, and we sailed to HemRidge. I was greeted with cheers when we reached the shore. I don't think I've ever been so happy to see so many Hemroys popping out to see me. They were usually just irritating, but today they handed me the rest of their gold.

I watched them unload the boxes and then unpack them. They held up the shields and tapped them with their knuckles. "These are incredibly light!" one proclaimed.

"I think they are magical," I said, not knowing.

"Let's test them out," said a leader of his men.

"Why waste time!" I proclaimed, then pointed toward the direction of Hicklewiess. "There's gold in them thar' hills!"

The Hemroy soldiers let out a loud battle cry and cheered. "We've been preparing for Operation Hemroy Relief for far too long," the leader shouted. "The time to apply it is now!"

"Preparation H, for short," one of them whispered to me after seeing my confused look.

With that said they all boarded the ship and took off towards Hickleweiss. I was very proud of myself for giving the Hemroys a little push, and however that they emerge from this would change history. I waved them off and headed to a small boat that was left for me on the shore. That's when I stopped and noticed a small label on one of the boxes. "100% Balsa". Robbie got me, again. Oh well, I thought. Things could be worse; I could be one of the dworcs right now.

Word around the Scuttlebutt Tavern the next day was that the Hemroy's were overrunning the warrior training camp and tried taking everyone down from a weakness in their rear flanks. The little dworc's didn't fare too well, as their shields caved in, though, and they were lanced out of existence.

<hr>

Entry 77

On my way through Cloverose, I stopped in for a short while at Lhentil Keep. Not much happens there, unless I'm around, so overall, it's a pleasant place to catch up on some rest and maybe do some shopping. I was on my way to Lucky's Coffee Shop, a place I had grown fond of in the Elven district. To my surprise, when I got there for my morning coffee and news scroll, I bumped into two fellow Red Crimson thieves giving the owner of the shop a hard time. Their names were Apichat and Onquay.

"Well, well, well," Apichat stated, as he saw me approach. "If it isn't old weasel bait!"

Onquay just giggled and nodded his head. I just grinned and brushed passed them, pocketing a few coins. "Just give me the usual, Storekeeper," I said, tossing one of their coins on the countertop. "...and keep the change."

It looked as though Lucky, the store owner, had been sweating profusely. The red haired halfling was being bullied by my old classmates. He answered me nervously, "Aye."

I looked back and noticed the two slime bags giving the halfling the evil eye. "What's going on boys?" I asked, leaning slightly on the counter, just enough so they could see my blade sticking out from under my cloak.

"Just a bit of strong-arming," Apichat replied, while slowly sipping his coffee.

"None of your business, brother," Onquay chimed in, his angry blue eyes nearly burning a hole through me.

"Red Crimsons don't bother with shopkeeps," I said, ignoring his intimidation tactic. "We go for big game. Besides, you utter piles of rat droppings, Lucky's Coffee Shop is my haunt, so scram."

Lucky lowered himself behind the counter and started whimpering. The two thieves approached me slowly. "Be a careful dog," Onquay spat. "We're working for Elfalfuh now. The new boss of the Elftown section of Lhentil Keep."

I didn't know any Elfalfuh. But, I could surmise, by his choice of hiring these two wet pair of socks, that he wasn't the sharpest tip of a spear. "Tell Elfalfuh there's a new boss in town," I said, while pointing at the shopkeeper. "Him!"

The shopkeeper's eyes got wide and then rolled back in his head as he passed out on the floor. "And I'm his second-in-command!" That being said, I grabbed Apichat's coffee and dumped it on his boot, before pulling my dagger and pointing it at them. They made a hasty retreat for the door, nearly tripping over one another. "Stay in the street, you dogs!" I warned.

"That ought to take care of them," I spoke to the passed out halfling lying on the floor. Feeling like I just did a good deed, I rewarded myself with a free refill before taking my news scroll and heading out. I love standing up to bullies like these for the shopkeepers. They don't understand that all you have to do is stand tough and never show any weakness.

I found a shady spot down the road under a tree, so I sat down and opened the scroll. "Hapless Shopkeepers Murdered by New Vicious Mob Boss" the headline read. Below the headline was the most scarred up drawing of the hugest Elf I had ever seen. He must have been the size of an ogre.

I did a spit take over the scroll and my trousers. The victim was a shopkeeper I'd defended the other day. I was a little upset, so I ended up just crumpling the scroll and throwing it into the trash. "Just great," I spoke out loud, mostly to myself. "Now, I have to go to the cleaners!"

When I arrived at the laundry shop, I kicked out two more thugs who were giving the shopkeeper a hard time. The owner yelled at me after the duo left. For a person in the cleaning business, he sure used a lot of unclean language. I decided that I would never go back to this guy, but it didn't matter, because I heard the business burned down a few days later.

<hr>

€nτry 78

Two of the most heroic, brave, and beautiful fighters in the Unremembered Realms are sisters who go by the names Sunshine and Moonbeam. Blonde-haired Sunshine and white-haired Moonbeam were rumored to have gotten trained by the best fighters in all the lands. They were famous for effortlessly slaughtering enemy males who got caught off guard by their beauty.

Of course, Sunshine and Moonbeam were out to get me, or I probably wouldn't have mentioned them. The Mayor of Mossborough hired the two to bring me to the courts...dead or alive. I'd managed to evade all of their attempts to capture me, until one day when I was trapped by a herd of Centicorns. It was near the city of Watercliff, just east of Brokenpoor. Centicorns are half human and half unicorn. They are usually quite peaceful and social, so I don't know why they were so angry at me. It was my partner, Aggression, who managed to get away with their sacred Hoof Heart gemstone.

I would have gotten away too, but I slipped in some Centicorn dung; which, by the way, does not smell of wildflowers and maple nuts like you'd assume. "Hoof hearted!" they'd cry out, in their broken common tongue as they cornered me. "Hoof hearted!"

"It wasn't me!" I laughed, "It's probably my boots you smell."

I don't think they got the joke. "Hoof hearted!" they'd repeat; I just giggled that much harder.

The rainbow colored horns sticking out of their foreheads were sharp, though, and they were not afraid to use them. After a short meeting and some nasty looks, I thought all hopes of negotiation were lost. It was at that moment that Sunshine and Moonbeam appeared. The beauties raced in on their steeds and picked me up, running me as fast as possible away from the angry herd.

Sunshine took Magurk off me right away and Moonbeam followed behind with a pistol bow aimed at my back. "We're going to get a big reward for you, handsome," Sunshine grinned.

I knew I was doomed. These lovely ladies were as intelligent and deadly as they were beautiful. If I had any hope of escape, I would have to seize any opportunity that presented itself. I held patiently onto Sunshine as she rode toward the main road to Mossborough. "What is that horrible smell?" she blurted out with a frown.

"I can smell it back here!" Moonbeam shouted, while pinching her nose.

"It's Centicorn dung," I said, as I lifted my boot. "I slipped in a pile of it earlier."

"Well, I can't ride too much longer with this," Sunshine replied. "It smells like road apple pie!"

"There's a dry cleaner in Brokenpoor," I suggested. "My dry cleaner, Pumice, can clean my clothes quicker than you can say Hoof Hearted."

Moonbeam giggled at the joke, but Sunshine didn't show any emotion at all. "This better not be a trick, rogue," she said, while pulling the horse reins in the direction of Brokenpoor.

"No tricks," I lied. "I have to pick up a hat I left there anyways."

When we got to the shop, I was glad to see a line queued up at the counter. It gave me a bit of hope. The two ladies guided me up, and Pumice met us with a big grin. "Is that what I think it is?" he asked, looking at my boots, as a bit of drool formed on the Bog-wizards lips.

The ladies could see he was a bit of a kook, so they stepped back in disgust as I bent down to remove one of my boots. "Oh," I paused and stood back up. "Were you able to get the bird business off my favorite hat?"

"Why, yes!" he said, pulling it out from below the counter. "It was delicious, I mean, difficult to clean. I hope you are pleased with the results!"

"I sure am," I said, as I took my magical Hat of Disguising and placed it on my head.

I turned around and said "Excuse me, ladies," but, they grabbed me by both arms. "Oh, excuse us, sir, we thought you were some-one else!"

I brushed passed them and out on the street. When I looked back, I could see Sunshine and Moonbeam inspecting the faces of all the customers in the shop. Too bad they didn't follow their nose. I was still wearing my smelly boots that I'm sure Pumice will give me a good price for cleaning. I wish I could have seen their faces when they discovered that I took their horses. I'm grateful Sunshine left Magurk in one of her packs.

Later, when I met up with Aggression at a tavern, which; shall remain nameless, I approached the table where he was sitting. "Hoof Hearted?" I asked.

"You caught me," he smirked, pulling the gem slightly out from under his cloak.

Entry 79

The worst part about adventuring is dealing with the egos of other adventurers. I cannot tell you how many times I've witnessed infighting within my group; I'm surprised that half the team doesn't get wiped out before we meet the first monster, or at least by the time we have to divide the first treasure. There's always a fighter who thinks he is the toughest or a wizard who thinks he is the most powerful. If you play your cards right, this can work out to your advantage.

For example, a town official by the name Setzer Barlow, once came running in a total panic through the tavern doors of the Flippenburg Tavern in a total panic. When he caught his breath, he started shouting about a band of Drigs who holed themselves up in a local mine owned by the Mayor of Shamptown.

Two giant fighters stood up from their table across the room and shouted: "If you want these Drigs flushed out, leave it up to us!" Their names were Killfest and Manglemud, the boldest fighters in the province of Thunderfuss.

Also standing up was Porkenthall the Windbag. This wizard was known for shooting his mouth off more than a cannon during Fallfest! While he was up bragging of his exploits to Setzer, I waved and gave Setzer a quick nod. The town official nodded back and said "Is there anyone else willing to step up for our beloved Shamptown?"

Healy, the cleric, was asleep sitting next to me, so I picked up his hand and waved it. Healy hated the fighters, so I found this to be quite the funny joke.

When we got to the mines, I could see that some Drigs had, indeed, taken up residence. What are Drigs, you ask? They are a mixed bag of races; some orc, human, and even elf mixed in, once in a while. They live the gypsy lifestyle and just go wherever the wind blows them. They are quite harmless, unless they get their eyes set on something – then it's a fight. You can't make friends with one, because they will try to mooch off of you, and if you do ever help them, they are hard to shake.

Around the outside of the mine was tattered clothing hung on laundry lines and a couple of old wagons that the Drigs were, obviously never going fix. They even painted new words under the Shamptown Mine sign, so now it read "Shamptown Mine, Not Yoors!" The few Drigs hanging around the front saw the small party approaching and immediately ran inside.

"They know why we're here," Manglemud stated. "Let's get to some killing!"

"I will slaughter them all," raged Killfest.

"Not before I fry them to a crisp!" Porkenthall yelled back.

The three paused, briefly, and then ran into the mouth of the mine, while Healy and I just casually sauntered forward. We knew that Drigs were easy to kill, but if you ever saw one, there's probably twenty more around the corner. We stood in the opening, for a moment, listening to the screams and slashing; the fiery explosions and howls of pain.

"Have you seen the fancy lockpicking set they've got in the window at the Shamptown flip-n-wink?" I asked Healy. "I heard it's enhanced with some magic."

"Yeah," he responded. "I guess some rogue had some big gambling debts. Poor chump."

"I heard it was Apichat, my old guild brother," I whispered.

"No way," Healy responded, shaking his head. "I thought he had loaded dice?"

"Had is the word," I said, pulling the dice from my pocket. "I was going to switch them back, but I changed my mind."

Screams echoed down through the shaft. Then, silence.

"Well," Healy said. "Time to go clean up!"

I put on my gloves and we started into the mine. Not far into it, we saw a large smoldering pile of Drig corpses. Sliced and stabbed ones had been scattered throughout the rest of the area.

The overwhelmed bodies of our companions were laying on the floor as well, overcome by the sheer number of Drigs. I never felt bad for adventurers like this. They would run headlong into danger, and more times than not, end up getting themselves or others killed. Healy and I learned not to be so impulsive and we have the gray hairs to prove it!

The cleric and I picked up the remaining valuables off the trio and yelled out for any remaining Drigs. A few popped out, cautiously waiting for us to attack. We gave them our fallen comrades gold and a magic dagger, in exchange for them leaving the mines for good. They agreed.

They had planned on moving out, anyway, because they had discovered a better cave with a waterfall not far away. If our impatient friends had thought about things and laid out a plan, they wouldn't be dead right now.

"Porkenthall is still alive," Healy said, as he waved his hands over the body. "I shouldn't heal this fool, but I will."

Healy was a kind soul, even when it came to helping those who don't deserve it. We propped Porkenthall against a wall and left him a couple of day's rations. Healy and I got a huge reward from Setzer Barlow back at Shamptown. It was more than enough for me pick up the magic lockpick set in Shamptown.

Entry 80

There is nothing worse than being cornered somewhere with some loudmouth adventurer who won't stop bragging about their hireling. I love adventuring and all the thrills of a quest, but when it comes to your hirelings, I couldn't care less.

Don't get me wrong, if we are on some quest, I don't mind knowing the hireling's skill set or what they're bringing to the party. But when I'm involved, there's something at stake. It's not so uncommon that the adventurer will give the hireling a magic item if it benefits the group. The problem is that the adventurer uses this act of generosity to embark on a bragging quest, which doesn't always end well for the braggart.

For example, I remember waiting patiently at the blacksmith's in the city of Brokenpoor. He was fixing something that I had broken, so I decided to relax in the waiting area for a bit. As I was thumbing through a worn out copy of "Blacksmith Quarterly," in walked Goiterchin the Half-Orc Cleric. Apparently, he had just come back from clearing out a kobold infestation in some old fort nearby.

In the treasure horde, he discovered a magical pair of bracers that were probably worth a fortune. Not having a lot of common sense, he gave them to Birdhelmet his hireling. The lucky grunt also snatched a sword from their recently deceased fighter, and some armor too. All Goiterchin kept was a cool magical cloak pin with a little flame on it. He told me it helped to protect him from fire.

I don't even know my hireling's names, most of the time; they are there to carry the heavier loot or be a gap stop in case I'm being chased. The trick is to never employ a hireling that can run faster than you. Whenever Goiterchin bragged, I just nodded my head, pretending to care, but all I could think about was getting out of there. About an hour later, the blacksmith appeared with my item, so I left as quickly as possible.

The next morning I hit the local Scarbucks coffee shop and was flipping through the morning news scrolls when I came across a headline that read: "Goiterchin the Cleric Mysteriously Murdered." Apparently, he was stabbed in the back and robbed of all of his goods. What a shame.

Years later I bumped into Birdhelmet at the Bucketswill Tavern in Daggersfoot. He vaguely remembered me, so he came over and said hello. It wasn't too long, before we started remembering Goiterchin and telling stories about the old coot. The former hireling even began to laugh at the lack of work that the constables did in investigating the murder. As he talked, he waved his hands around, momentarily exposing the dead cleric's magical pin from underneath a flap in his cloak.

After I had gone to the counter to get us some food, Birdhelmet started to complain about Goiterchin between bites. Especially, about how Goiterchin was too trusting of people that he hardly knew, and how easily tricked he was. Minutes later, the backstabbing hireling came down with a mysterious case of food poisoning. When he finally stopped throwing up in the latrine, I drug the stumbling fool to a local paladin named Dewgood McGee, to whom I owed a favor. The paladin received a promotion for solving the case; while I got a nifty cloak pin that helps protect me from fire.

Entry 81

Off the River Vile is an underground dungeon called Floptover. At the time I was there, it was run by an old wizard, named Gerinthall. Once a day, every day, Gerinthall would use some dark magic to drain his victim's life force to keep himself alive longer.

Like a fool, I decided to join a brave band of soon-to-be corpses and see how much treasure I could loot from this old man; without being caught. We were only a couple of levels into the place when my group got captured. The druid in our party had a tizzy and started yelling when he saw the bugbear guardians weren't recycling or some nonsense. I was thinking about stabbing this druid, myself, but out from the shadows crept Gerinthall, himself. He mustn't have noticed me, because I was in full blend mode in my magic cloak when he levitated into the room. He had energy beams shooting from his fingertips, which sucked the life forces out of my companions. I watched, in shock, as their drained corpses hit the floor.

I thought our druid would be pleased about this, for he wasn't just killed and left to rot, but his life force would be used to sustain another being for a day. After draining them, the wizard turned to me, his eyes were pitch black, and he had some drool spatter from his lips. "What is that I smell? You think you can hide with magic? You're next, rogue," he said, as he signaled his two bugbear henchmen. "You'll be my midnight snack."

The wizard must have been pretty confident, because he never searched me. The two ugly bugbears took me into a room and threw me into a cell with iron bars. I noticed there was another cell attached, and sitting in it, was a bard slowly strumming his lute.

"You must be on the snack list, too," he spoke to me, as he looked up.

"Yeah," I responded, lowering my cowl. "And what are you?"

"I was supposed to be dinner for the bugbears, but my songs calm the old man's nerves," he answered. "Who are you?"

"My name doesn't matter," I said, while testing the bars for weaknesses.

"Well, my name is Trousers. I'm a bard," he explained. "People called me that, because of my colorful pants."

He reached through the bars to shake my hand, so I responded just the same. "Nice to meet you, fancy pants."

After the introduction, I pulled out my lock picks. "It's no use," Trousers points out. "Magically locked."

I spent a while going through my gear trying to figure a way to work something out to facilitate my escape. The last thing I wanted, was to end up as a bad case of gas for some old kook who should have kicked the bucket a century ago. As I sat there thinking, Trousers played some songs, which were quite good.

That's when I noticed he was using his music to transform objects in his cell. His dinner plate became a clock; his sword became a bouquet of flowers. "How do you do that?" I asked.

"Oh, it's just a polymorph spell set to a tune," he replied.

"Transform yourself into a rat or something and escape!" I blurted out.

"I've tried on myself, but it never works," he replied. "I've never tried it out on another living thing, though, I've never had the training."

"I have an idea," I said.

Not long after that, the two bugbear guards came into the room, only to find Trousers playing his lute and a small black and white cat. "The other one has escaped," they shouted in unison. "Where is the other prisoner, bard?" They demanded to know.

Trousers just laughed and kept playing. The angry bugbears opened the cell door and dragged the bard out, who was followed by the little cat. They took him into the bedroom of Gerinthall, who was pacing in front of his bed.

"Sing to me, bard," he said. "I can't seem to sleep again. All these life forces gave me the worst indigestion..."

That's when he noticed the cat. "A kitty!" He said excitedly and knelt down. He picked up the purring cat and sat on his bed. "I love kitties! Their fur is so soft. I think I'll name you, Agamemnon."

Trousers sat down in a chair and played. This time he started to sing a sleep spell. The two bugbears fell asleep and crumpled to the floor. It had no effect on Gerinthall though, he immediately recognized the traitor's activity and started to raise his hands. The minute he did that, I unpolymorphed from the cat back into myself and rammed Magurk through his stomach. "Sorry to kill your appetite, geezer," I said in his face. "And by the way, before you die, I want you to know I used your ancient spell book as a litter box!"

Entry 82

Off the west coast of the Unremembered Realms is a large city, called Tidepool. They call it that, because the ocean in front of the city is a swirling pool of certain death. Sailors from all over the realms have been sucked down into it and were never seen alive again.

Why go there, you ask? Well, because of the pool. Certain water springs up in places around the city. The water comes up through cracks in the rocks, and sometimes they spring up as geysers on the mainland. Once in a while, a ship will go down, and a bit of treasure will ride the current up through the cracks. Quite a lucky find for a relaxing vacationer who's wading around in the warm water. On the flip side, it's not too fun when the head of a dead sailor pops up either.

Because of these warm water geysers, Tidepool has become a luxury city with hotels popping up around these refreshing springs. The city is mostly run by the elves, and it is easily the best place to go to relax on the west coast of Farlong. They are open to a variety of other races and creatures as well, so you have to be on your toes.

I just so happened to be visiting there after a squad of soldiers from Lhentil Keep decided I should be arrested. It had something to do with the ultra-rare magical amulet I found at the Magic Item Reserve & Trust that they thought was heavily guarded.

I managed to get away relatively easily, thanks to my Speed Boots. I also noticed that when I was wearing the amulet, I didn't seem to need any sleep or rest. While the pursuing squad made their camp, I wandered through the Hoktu Mountains, even finding the time to visit Desperation Point, the popular suicide spot for spurned lovers. It was a beautiful view from the top, but I figured the bottom was probably a mess.

I walked for about four day,s until I got to Tidepool. It wasn't long before the upscale resort town had drained all my gold and I was getting pretty hungry. I headed out to the local flip-n-wink to do a bit of selling. The owner's name was Shifty Kibbles, and he was this greasy dog faced Gnoll who wore these garish clothes and never seemed to stop smiling. I decided I had liked the amulet, but I liked to eat even more, so we negotiated a decent price and I handed it over to him.

For some reason, when I took it off, I got fatigued. I took some of my new coins and rented a nice hut with a little swimming hole. I immediately fell asleep, and it lasted for three days. When I woke up, I headed back down to Shifty's, only to find out that he'd been spotted around town wearing the amulet. When the Lhentil Keep guards showed up, they tried to arrest him for the robbery. Shifty ran and managed to escape on a small rowboat. That didn't work out, though. He decided to stay close to the shore, I heard, but it wasn't long before the swirling pool of death pulled him in. The guards witnessed the whole thing and went back to their room at the resort empty handed, obviously knowing all hope of the amulet's return was lost.

And how right they were! As I relaxed in the pool by my small hut, a little geyser sprang up, along with bits of Kibble and the amulet. I picked up the priceless treasure from the water, placed it around my neck and went to the central office complaining my room smelled like wet dog.

Seeing the amulet around my neck, they thought I was a high-roller, so they comped me a free room, with all expenses paid for a week; which, was much larger and nicer. Apparently, they had to move out some recently fired soldiers, who were forced to make do in my old hut.

Entry 83

I can still remember the day I met my sister for lunch at the local tavern. I thought she was acting a bit odd when I stopped by her place in Shallowditch. My brother-in-law, Stan, was doing good after his promotion down at the local Path Finders Union. They are responsible for maintaining the paths in Farlong that travelers use. Apparently, he'd been promoted to sign holder; he'd hold up caravans for hours he confessed to me with a grin.

I thought my sister would be in good spirits, but instead, she had some dreadful news. "It's your nephew, Stan Jr," she explained, while picking over her salad. "You need to talk to him."

I thought Stan Jr was a good kid, a little weird, but with a good heart. "What's the matter," I asked. "Did he skip school again? I've told you before that all teenagers do that."

"No, no, no," she said, starting to weep. "Jr. decided to change his name to Ficus Hugsafern; my boy wants to become a druid!"

I spat out my food and nearly fell out of my seat, but my sister was fast and caught me before I fell over. I was shocked, to say the least; I had not seen this coming. Was I not there enough for him when he was younger? Was he corrupted by the Farlong Education Administration? All these questions went through my mind. After I had got myself together, she told me more about his behavior.

"At first, he started talking to animals like a common ranger," she explained. "So we thought, well, I guess that's okay, even though we hoped for more. We had planned he'd become a Path Finder, like his father, but he said that was square!"

"It's when he started talking to plants that we knew something was wrong," she continued. "He started wearing bell bottom robes and hanging around an alchemist, named Bugwagon."

I had heard enough at this point and decided to find Stan Jr and administer some tough love. My sister told me "Ficus" and "Bugwagon" liked to hold protests at a local flower shop. By the time I got there, the shopkeeper was trying to shoo a young group of druids away from the building. They were holding signs that read "These roses are red, with blood!", "Bouquet? No way!", and "Beware the Tulip Smack!"

Stan Jr. nearly knocked me over when the shopkeeper started dowsing them with water buckets. I grabbed his arm and slowly walked him down a side alley. "Uncle?", he asked, in surprise. "What are you doing here?"

"What are you doing here, Stan?", I returned the question.

"I've found something to believe in. I think I can change the Realms, to do my part," he started to drone on. "The Realms are full of violence and desperation. If we could all just live together with all the different creatures, there would be no more fear. We could dance amongst the trees and eat only what the plants are willing to share!"

"I've gone on dungeon raids with druids, Stan, I've seen them cast plant spells that kill," I reminded him. "Even a smelly druid needs to eat."

He started babbling on with some nonsense about trees, bees, and fleas. Some rhetoric that he must memorize, probably fed to him by some goof at the Druid Academy, but then, a light came on in my head.

"It's a girl isn't it?" I asked.

My nephews face turned red, and he hung his head. "Yes, Uncle."

A huge weight lifted off my shoulders. I just smiled. "What's the girl's name, boy?"

"It's Starchime," he said, lifting his head back up. "She's pretty as all get out, and she's really into all this junk."

There was the nephew I knew. We talked for a while and straightened things out. His persona of Ficus was just a ruse to steal the girl's heart. It's not something I would have even considered, but I can respect the chase of a great treasure. He is, after all, my blood.

Entry 84

I was once betrothed to a female thief, named Kim Chee. She was the granddaughter of Pilfur Ing, one of the greatest rogues to come out of the Jade Garden Thieves Guild. Kim and I met at a conference of the Guilds that Pilfur was hosting on their small eastern island of Po Gai, which is a stone's throw off the coast between Gaspenfall and Darkmist.

I was sitting next to her in a breakout session on lock picking; I was pretending to be asleep, while she drew funny pictures of the speaker. We hung around the whole conference together after that, walking, joking, and falling into an emotional state that some would consider love.

Pilfur took a shine to me as well, even offering not to kill me if I left her alone. While he made plans for my death, Kim and I did some adventuring. Exploring dungeons, gutting monsters, getting the tar beat out of us by ogres; it was a grand time indeed.

The problem was Kim Chee was tired of this way of life. She had a heart for thieves, because of her grandfather, but that's pretty much where it ended.

One night, as our party sat around the campfire cleaning orc blood off of our blades, I noticed her beautiful face in the firelight. Her almond shaped eyes, her lips as she spat at the druid sitting next to her, and the way she picked orc brains from her hair so daintily. I knew, then and there, that she deserved better.

She smiled at me and walked over. "I think I deserve better," she said. "I'm sick of smelling like orc brains."

Kim left the next day to go back to Po Gai, while I continued adventuring with the group. I have to admit that I miss her sometimes. To this day, whenever I'm plunging Magurk through the eye socket of some smelly orc, or spitting on a druid, I think of her.

Entry 85

Just east of the Barrendry desert I found a little oasis with some fresh water and palm trees with some fruit. I hung out for a day, because it seemed kind of peaceful. As I sat soaking my feet in the fresh water pool, I heard a noise from behind me.

I whirled around to see a two-foot high creature with tan fur and two doe-like eyes that instantly disarmed my fear. It was so cute! I'd never before seen a little humanoid creature like this. It looked at me with a partially toothed grin, then toddled over and took my human hand.

It cooed and garbled, as it led me through some brushes and around some trees. It wasn't long before I saw a little ramshackle house that blended very well with its surroundings. Out in the yard were a couple of more of these creatures. When they saw me coming, they ran up and hugged my legs.

Normally I'd be more cautious, but these creatures seemed so defenseless I could not see them as untrustworthy. They guided me up to the front door and ushered me through it. Inside the room, it was pure chaos. Dishes, clothes, toys, papers – you name it. Everywhere, there was one of these creatures climbing, playing, laughing, or jumping.

Behind a big desk, in the center of the room was an old wizard with his face planted firmly on the desk with his fingers interlocked over the back of his hair. Once I stepped inside, all the creatures cheered. That's when the bleary-eyed wizard looked up from his desk. He rubbed his eyes and said, "I, I....think I know you..."

He was right. He did know me. I started to say "You're Gerbernoob the Great, the Keeper of Mindmaps, the Bloodspiller, the..."

"...all gone!" He wept. "That wizard is long gone."

"What happened? The last time I saw you, you were putting a lightning bolt through the king of the Hoktu Hill Giants!"

"Those days were fun, weren't they?" He seemed to remember fondly. At that moment, one of the creatures pinched another one, and it started to wail loudly. If either the wizard or I talked, it would only cry louder, so we couldn't. I picked up the crying creature and held it until it stopped sobbing. The other creatures just kept playing, like nothing happened.

"What are these things?" I asked. The little creature I was holding started to fall asleep.

"They are called Patterlings," he explained. "They are like toddlers; only they stay like this forever."

Gerbernoob read my face and started answering my question before I could even ask it. "There was this old, crazy witch, by the name of Materna, who used to live here. She wanted to have a baby her whole life, but she was horribly ugly and smelly, so she hid herself here in this oasis to perfect her magic."

"Apparently, she was successful in making these things," I said, looking about the place.

"She was," he continued. "The only problem was she used these rare magical gems to make the creatures. I had heard at a pub in Brokenpoor of a crazy witch with magical gems, so I couldn't resist coming here to take a shot at taking them from her."

"So, there was a battle?" I asked. "Obviously, you won."

"I wouldn't say that, now," Gerbernoob admitted. "Once I incinerated her, these creatures saw me as their new mom, and they follow me wherever I go!"

"Why not just sneak out?" I advised, but he just frowned.

"I've tried that," he said, shaking his head. "No matter where I go or what I do, they magically appear – there is no escape! I don't sleep at night, I can't keep this house clean, and I've totally given up on adventuring! The only way out is death."

He said "death" like it was a good word. "How long have you been doing this?" I inquired.

"Ten long years," he started to cry, "Please, my friend, put me out of my misery!"

"That's not my way," I stated. "You've made your bed."

"I know I have," he yelled at me. "And they keep messing it up!"

Three of the little creatures laughed, as they jumped up and down on his bed. Gerbernoob reached into the desk drawer and pulled out two large handfuls of what looked like priceless gems. "Here, you can take all these!" He offered.

I was stunned by their beauty. I stepped forward and almost touched one. "You can have all the gems, if you could just pattersit for me for an hour," Gerbernoob explained. "I just have to run to the supply store in Brokenpoor for some milk.

It sounded easy enough. "Sure," I said, staring at the gems. "Just let me grab my boots, I left them by the water."

Gerbernoob nearly fell over with joy. He started to explain all the instructions of how to care for the Patterlings should something come up. He was also loading up a backpack with scrolls, potions, and a spell book. "Go on, feel free to pocket those gems," he said looking hopeful.

"I left my lucky money purse with my boots," I lied. "Just give me two minutes."

As I walked away from the little house, the patterlings gathered around the wizard as they all watched me walk toward the water. When I looked back, they were still smiling and waving. Gerbernoob was holding up a gem, so I could see it clearly. After I had put my Speed Boots on, I grabbed my gear and ran so fast away from there that I could barely hear the fading sobs of the old wizard, as he yelled after me.

Entry 86

When I was a kid, I used to love to go into the Palm Eye Finger Magic Shop. My parents would drop my kid sister and me there when they wanted to get their shopping done around town. We were starry-eyed youths and had big dreams of shooting fireballs or lightning bolts at some ferocious dragon someday. Getting hordes of treasure wasn't a far distant thought for me either.

Bub and Lar were the owners of the store and loved showing kids their latest inventions. Bub, a kindly old magic user, would always greet us with a warm smile, then run over and get us with his famous "pull my finger" trick. That always grossed out my sister, but I chuckled. His business partner, Lar, was more subdued, but he would wave us over to see his latest magical invention or found items.

One day, Lar was showing us some of his new magic cards; a whole deck that did many things when a card was drawn. That's when a druid stormed into the shop in quite the huff. The interruption and rudeness of this man are a strong memory for me, or maybe it was his awful body odor. I almost ran over and pulled

Bub's finger, just to cover the smell!

The druid was on a rant about some defective magic item that he had apparently bought here at the shop and was threatening to bring legal action if the two old men didn't close their doors. I don't remember exactly what the item was that had him so twisted, but I noticed that I could see his underpants through the burned out hole in the back of his robes.

"It's a bummer," he yelled. "Just look at me!"

Bub, Lar, and us kids just laughed as he danced around showing us the damage from the defective item. "Come now, Muckstraw," Bub said while chuckling. "You must learn to turn the other cheek!"

With everyone now laughing hysterically, Muckstraw shook his fist at the wizards and ran out of the door. We all snickered for a bit and went back to listening about the deck of magical cards. "I've been experimenting on these cards, " Lar explained. "Some cards give amazing results when picked, and the others...well, not so good. Come back in a week or two, and I'll have all the bugs worked out."

So, we left. After a week, I decided to go back to see how Lars deck of magical cards were coming along. When I approached the shop, I saw that the entire place looked like chaos. Giant burn holes were in the ground and man-eating plants had grown and were sticking out of what was left of a window. Law enforcement were shooing people away from the place. I remember asking one of them what happened.

"A bunch of druids came in after hours and apparently got ahold of some magical deck of cards," he said, while looking down at me. "This whole mess is the result of that. You probably don't want to hang around here, kid. Some of the druids have gone mad and are trashing the city."

I'm glad the two old wizards weren't there; at least they were safe. I snuck around the constable to get a better look at the shop. Lying next to some burning debris, was a playing card. I cautiously walked over and picked it up. When I flipped over the card and looked at the picture, it was a Jack with a red diamond on it. The card lifted off my hand, slightly, and started to glow green. After only a few seconds, the card dissipated into thin air, while the glow fell gently on my hand.

From that point on, I dreamed of being a rogue, becoming more agile, and getting comfortable within the shadows. I became the master of Hide and Sneak. Picking apart locks was like a game for me; the harder the challenge, the better. I don't know if that card was a curse or a blessing. I suppose I'm still trying to figure it all out.

<hr />

Entry 87

Do you want to know what a bad idea is? Opening a store that sells thieving supplies. When I was a student at the Red Crimson Guild, I made friends with a fellow lizard man student by the name of Peyton Stockmore. His big dream was to open a store just like that. I had my doubts about it, but he was convinced he'd make a fortune.

After graduation, Peyton bought a local shop that had been abandoned by some elves who ran a fast food joint out of it. Nobody likes Elven cuisine, not even the elves, so that was bound to fail.

Peyton spent his life savings on stocking up his store with all of the latest gear and gadgets that a thief would ever need. He was grinning ear to ear on opening day, but that was not going to last. You see, his first day was also his last. The number of customers was enormous, and items were flying off the shelves. The problem was that nobody was paying for any of it because they were all thieves.

"But, I put up a 'No Stealing' sign!" he lamented, looking over his empty shelves. "I guess I was just born to fail!"

It wasn't long before we were on our way to Desperation Point up in the Hoktu Mountains. Poor Peyton had given up all hope. I went along to talk him out of it – to help him understand that he could use his talents for the greater good, like stealing treasure that would make us both rich! Eventually, we reached Lhentil Keep and stopped at a tavern to eat. It was a dump, called the Sidebucket; which, provided a complimentary bucket and breath mint with each meal. "So much for my last meal," he moaned, holding his stomach.

We eventually stopped at a general store, because we needed some climbing gear to get up to Desperation Point. My depressed friend bought a rope with a few of the copper coins that we had left. "At least it was affordable," I said, trying to cheer up Peyton. "They should charge more, so you don't have to sail to your death with a pocket full of coins."

Peyton stopped in his tracks, then looked at me with a big grin. "You just gave me a brilliant idea! Follow me!"

Within hours he was talking to some construction workers, food vendors, and some mercantile shops. It was only about two weeks before Peyton opened up his new store, "Leaping Lizards Last Minute Supply Shop & Restaurant." Peyton deducted that if you're going to leap to your doom, why not have a nice last meal, then spend the rest of your cash on some quality duds for the trip down.

The business was a smashing success. The food was to die for, and many customers fell in love, although shortly, with the excellent customer service. It's nice to know that I could help out a friend with a little push in the right direction.

Entry 88

One time, while in a tavern in the Realm of Gaspenfall, I was doing a bit of gambling and upset a gang of dwarves known as "The Black Willows." This group of low-heights was led by a dwarf named Quade, and he was the worst gambler I'd ever seen. The bearded chump was going crazy because he couldn't figure out how I kept flipping his magical Coin of Cheating. I had heard about this item before, so I used my minor telekinesis power to flip the coin back over when it landed in his favor.

We spent a few hours playing cards, dice, and coins, but whatever game the frustrated Black Willows tried, they would always lose. I could tell their ire was up when they drew their weapons, so I grabbed their coin from mid-air, while I flipped the table over and ran. I hated leaving all of my winnings, but I used the table full of falling gold pieces as a distraction to escape. "Our coin!" Quade shouted. "Find our special coin!"

While The Black Willows were distracted, I slipped out the back door and headed for a different tavern, so I could lay low. Dirtspill was a large city, and it had a plethora of different establishments in which I could hide. It was a tough town too; tavern brawls were common, and sometimes, even bet on.

I ducked into a place a few streets down, called the Rumblegut Tavern. It was busy, as always. If you were here, it was for food, fighting, or fun; which, in this place, could all be combined. Word of my presence got out, and it attracted the attention of the slime bag Mayor, Iva Bigfib. It wasn't long before this sleazy politician was sitting across the table from me and proposing some work. I've done small jobs for him before, so I listened, as he explained his situation.

Apparently, this was an election year, and his opponent in the race was a feisty elven lady, named Arabella Barkovich. She had gained popularity around the town for being tough, but honest. Bigfib found out he was down in the polls, so he wanted me to dig up some dirt on this Barkovich character.

Iva drew me a map and showed me the location of Arabella's campaign headquarters. Barkovich's staff consisted of volunteers who got little or no pay, because the spirited elf wasn't in anyone's pocket. Her headquarters was in a place known as "The Watering Gate," which was just west of town and away from the lights of the city.

Iva gave me a platinum piece and promised me more if I returned with the info. "If you don't find something," he warned. "You're going to be the one with dirt on you...literally!"

Any which way I could, I had to find something on this elven upstart, or I would be in trouble, for sure. By the time I reached the Barkovich headquarters, it was pretty late. Picking the door lock was easy, so I slipped in and started going through all of her notes. I didn't find much. The pointy-eared optimist seemed to be on the up-and-up and even had a few speeches written where she honored Iva and his accomplishments. Arabella ended the tribute with a statement that although he accomplished many things, it was time for him to move on. According to her notes, the campaign was low in funds so she had her doubts that she would make it. I started feeling sorry about what I was doing for that weasel mayor, so I reached into my pocket and grabbed the two coins; the platinum and the Magic Coin of Cheating. I dropped the platinum into a contribution bin and left, pocketing the Cheating Coin, which I wouldn't want to part with.

I headed back to the Rumblegut to tell Iva what a dirtbag he was. I knew he would be mad, but I didn't care. I felt pretty good about my decision. When I got there, the tavern keeper quickly dispatched a messenger to fetch the mayor. I must have nodded off for a moment, because when I woke up, I was staring into the faces of the angry Black Willows standing on the other side of my table. "Great to see you guys," I said, groggily. "Shall we play a game?"

"You know why we're here, thief," Quade spat, as he unsheathed his short sword and held it's razor sharp tip to my throat. "I don't know how you out-cheated me, but we've decided to tear you limb-from-limb!"

Before I could say anything, the mayor burst through the door. "Wait!" he yelled. "Don't kill him, yet!"

The dwarves all turned to see the mayor running towards us in his pajamas; he was short of breath from his quick sprint over. "Tell me, thief, what did you find out?"

"I didn't find any sign of corruption," I told him, as I reached in my pocket. "Barkovich has my vote."

Bigfib's face turned beet red, and he hissed at me, "I paid you to find out dirt, not backstab me! Give me my coin back, you scoundrel!"

"Here," I replied while picking the coin from my pocket. "What's yours is yours!"

When I slid the coin over the table exposing it as the Coin of Cheating, all the dwarves looked at it, then glanced at Quade. The leader had now turned to Bigfib, who had now grown horribly pale. "It isn't mine, I swear!" were the last words I heard, as I snuck out the back. Later, I found out Arabella had won the election by a landslide; which, is easy to do when your opponent has gone to pieces!

Entry 89

One day, as I was strangling Robbie the Thief, a small scroll fell from his pocket. I was curious about it, so I dropped him to the floor to pick it up. I don't know why I didn't finish off the crooked little halfling; I'd been tracking him for months. I finally caught up with Robbie outside a dumpy rental unit on the north end of Miftenmad.

"What is this?" I asked, showing him the note.

"It's a map to the greatest treasure in Farlong!" Robbie said coarsely, rubbing his neck. "And it's not for sale!"

I pocketed the note and turned away. "Now we're even for all the bogus maps you've sold me in the past," I said over my shoulder.

Robbie was trying to shout something to me, but couldn't raise his voice, on account of the strangulation, so I took off running. He couldn't catch his breath fast enough and I lost him quickly. I hid behind some crates in a dark alley and unrolled the little scroll. It was a neat little map with the word's "Behold Her Dating Service" on it.

So Robbie was seeking a mate. That must be what he meant by saying the greatest treasure! He was bitten by the love bug. I almost felt sorry for taking this, but the longer I thought about it, the more my curiosity grew. I knew halflings were kind of kooky when it came to romance, so I decided to see the little swindler's dream gal, or thing, for myself.

According to the map, he needed to go to Bellowmoon today and meet her by the infamous Forbidden Cave. That seemed odd to me, because the Forbidden Cave was named one of the most dangerous places in all of the Unremembered Realms. Many people have lost their lives around there. Against better judgment, I decided to pay Robbie's soon-to-be girlfriend a visit.

Most of the journey was extremely dangerous; the woods crawled with lycanthropes who like to eat humans for breakfast. I set out for Bellowmoon anyway, because I am pretty good friends with Two Chairs the Werewolf. I can't tell you how many times I've saved that overweight, hairy savage.

Miftenmad wasn't too far away from Bellowmoon, so I was able to make it over in just a few hours at a decent trot. The only natural obstruction was a piranha infested river; which, ran in front of the now abandoned Whitestone Castle. They call it the Slippenslider River, because of the slick mud along the bank that has sent many a traveler to their doom. The long dead king of Whitestone had commissioned a bridge to be built, but all that remained, these days, was a rickety rope bridge. The bridge was only about five feet above the water, so you can see the hungry, unblinking piranha fish below the surface, just waiting for you to fall in.

When I got to the Forbidden Cave, I noticed the skulls, bones, and some burn marks all around the entrance. The smell was acidic too; it reminded me of the way Whitestone Castle reeked, as it rotted away like a discarded meal. I pinched my nose and shouted, "Hello! I'm looking for the Behold Her girl!"

Immediately, I heard a loud belch, and some thunderous foot-steps coming from inside the cave. "Is that you, Robbie? Are you here for our date?"

Around the corner came an eight-foot tall creature with one eye and a mop-like mess on top of its head. She was completely round in the middle and she almost seemed to float over the ground, as she approached me. I swear, her gaze turned me to stone, because I couldn't seem to move or look away.

Her dress was a combination of different beddings that were roughly sewn together. I couldn't tell if the stains were dirt or blood. "My, my, my, handsome," she exclaimed, with a gap-toothed grin. "You look good enough to eat!"

Her breath shook me out of my paralysis and I ran and slid be-tween her hairy legs, as she made a grab for me. I circled back and made a dash for the bridge. Even with my fast magical boots, this Behold Her girl was keeping up the pace. "Bring back those sweet lips, Robbie!" she yelled. "So, I touched up my profile drawing a teensy weensy bit! You lied too – you said you were shorter!"

By the time she made that statement, I was already on the bridge. I knew she couldn't cross it with her girth, so I stopped on the other side. She immediately dove into the water and started to swim across the river. I watched, in amazement, as the piranha started in after her, but I was in more amazement when she began eating the killer fish! She began gulping them down hand over fist. She winked at me, as the fish blood spurted out of her mouth and ran down her chin over the thick black moles and wart stubble. "Look, Robbie! I'm catching us some dinner!" she said, between bites.

"Meet me at the cave," I shouted to her, "I'll be back with some candles, my darling!"

With that, said I ran back to Miftenmad, only to find Robbie sulking in the Scabdover Tavern. I walked up and threw the scroll on the table in front of him. "You certainly hit the jackpot this time Robbie, " I told him. "Your Behold Her girl is back at the Forbidden Cave; she wants to have you for dinner!"

Robbie the Thief looked like he had just won a contest. "Thank you!" he replied, with a big smile, "I didn't think you'd come back! Especially after all the tricks I've pulled on you in the past."

"Just don't be crumby to that elegant lady," I warned. "I have a feeling, that in her gut, your heart will be more than satisfactory."

The love-struck halfling hugged my leg, then ran out the door. I would've felt sorry for what I did, but the little slime swiped my money pouch when he hugged me. If love doesn't kill Robbie, I will.

Entry 90

I was tied up to a torture rack inside the secret hideout of the Bludfungus Bandits. I fell victim to one of their raids as I traveled through the Simplecon Valley with a caravan delivering some microchips; which, are a delicacy in the Unremembered Realms. Microchips are little vegetable crisps made by wood faeries, who dwell in the Faerwood Forest.

The bandits attacked us in a haphazard fashion, so a lot of my fellow travelers escaped. The Bludfungus leader, Axel Bludfungus, had captured me and was torturing me for information on where I thought the others might have run off to.

It wasn't long before a bandit scout returned to give the leader a report. "Did you find the microchips?" Bludfungus shouted at the clearly shaky underling.

The underling shook his head, no. The other bandits in the lair stepped back in fear. "You have failed in your mission!"

With that statement, the timid bandit was impaled through the chest with the leader's longsword. His body fell to the floor in a bloody heap. "Did he just kill his henchman?" I whispered to the guard next to me. "Does he always do that?"

The guard slowly nodded his head. "How do you know you're not next? Is everyone here so out of it that you can't see that you might be the victim of one of his bad moods," I whispered.

Axel pointed at the guard I had just whispered to and said, "You're the new leader," before leaving through a door. "Listen here, short straw," I whispered, again, "I wouldn't stick around this psycho too much longer. Your days are numbered!"

"But, but he failed his mission..." Shortstraw mumbled.

"Did you get murdered in school when you failed a math exam?!" I told him. "It's evident that guy didn't know what he was doing, but he just learned a lesson, so much for gaining wisdom."

I couldn't see the guards face, only his eyes through the helmet. You could tell my words were starting to sink in. "How many of your friends has he killed in the last three months?" I asked quietly.

"Ten or eleven," he replied.

"How many people has he killed during a robbery?" I asked, again.

"We do most of the killing..." he stated. "But, he has only killed two."

"Do the math," I told him. "Whose side is this guy on?"

The guard was counting on his fingers for a minute. It's a good thing they hadn't killed people who failed at math exams, I thought to myself, this fool would have been dead a long time ago. The bandit guard walked away from me to some other guards and started talking. Soon, the rest of them were trying to count on their fingers.

When Axel came back into the room, he walked up to me with a big grin. "I think your time is just about up, rogue!" he said, while unsheathing his sword.

"Can I ask a question?" I started, looking at the tip of his sword between my eyes.

"Hurry up, rag man, caravans just don't rob themselves, you know," he said.

"You just killed one of your troops for failing his mission," I stated.

"Yeah, so? He was obviously useless," the big guy answered.

I leaned forward a bit, until his sword point touched my forehead and I looked him straight in the eye. "Well, wouldn't that make you useless? Your mission was to capture all of the treasure, and it hasn't been done. It seems to me that your poor leadership is the reason for that young guard's demise and the lack of splittable treasure!"

Axel looked at me with a big frown, like he was trying to process the information. That's when he noticed his six remaining troops surrounding himself. Axel quickly laid down his sword and put his hands up. "Listen, guys; this common thief is a fool, a trickster. Don't listen to him!"

"He'll kill any one of you the next time you fail," I reminded them. "I'd rather be a fool than sword fodder. This coward won't even do the dirty work himself, unless it's cutting your throats!"

Shortstraw stepped up to Axel and said, "Hey boss, what's seven minus one?"

Axel remained quiet for a minute, thinking about the answer. The guards didn't wait for a reply and attacked him, cutting him to pieces on the spot. "It's five, you creep!" Shortstraw yelled, as he bashed on the body of his former boss.

"It's six, actually," I blurted out. That's when the now bloodthirsty guards turned toward me.

"I meant five; you're right...," I declared so that I wouldn't get stabbed.

Shortstraw turned to his men and proclaimed, "We are a new team of bandits. We shall now be called The Shortstraw Five!"

All six of them cheered and ran around the room celebrating. They didn't know math, but the bandits were nice enough to let me go. I don't know what happened to them after that, but let's hope they don't multiply.

€ntry 91

I was hanging out at the Greenbelly Tavern and heard a rumor that the Ivoryskull Dungeon in Dragonshelm was well organized for campaigning. From the indoor plumbing to the various snack tables that they have peppered along the corridors. I heard it made dungeon delves a memorable experience. Maybe it is because they went union. I had never been in a unionized dungeon before, so I was curious.

A short time later, I had snuck into the dungeon and back-stabbed a fairly notorious orc captain who was causing a lot of ruckus in some nearby villages. His troops were growing in strength, so the villagers hired me to off the leader in hopes of stopping a full-on invasion.

After offing the boss, I crept over to the barracks to eliminate a few of his crew. I was just about to stab a sleeping orc, but I let out a little noise that woke up the whole place up. That was just great. What a time for the call of nature. Before the orcs could grab their swords, I dove out of the room and ran down the hallway to the nearest bathroom. I had the worst food at Greenbelly's Tavern the night before, so I guess I shouldn't be too shocked that it was playing a number on my stomach.

I called a "time out, " but the orcs were not listening, at all. So, I locked the bathroom door and sat down in one of the nicest dungeon bathrooms I had ever seen. A little kobold stood in place holding a towel and every few moments would sprinkle some potpourri.

The orcs pounded on the door and shouted things that I didn't understand; I'm sure it wasn't nice, though. They left, for a moment, then came back with a small desk they could use to smash down the door. Lucky for me, the tea time chimes went off, and the orcs stopped bashing on the door and left for refreshments. Ivoryskull Dungeon is under very strict union control, so not taking a tea break would be a violation of their contract. I could tell they were angry about leaving me there, but what could they do?

I finished up, washed my hands, and tipped the little kobold who held out the drying towel for me. "Thanks for not letting them in," I said.

"Not my job," he snorted.

€ntry 92

Tax time in the Realms is a pretty tricky business. Nobody wants to pay them. It's even harder to find someone who wants to collect them! Fleecing the farmers is not that tough, but going after Throatslicer the Insane for his gold is a whole other story.

Leaders have tried everything to get powerful citizens to pay, which usually ends up in the death of the collector. It takes a pretty big fool to sign up for the task, and believe me; there's plenty of them.

The King of Gaspenfall was after me for years of back taxes. I'm not an easy guy to catch up with, so they set a trap in a cave outside of Daggerfoot. They were clued in on my whereabouts by my associate, Aggression the Thief, who spilled the beans on me.

Most of the time, my income is not taxable, because of my chosen profession. I don't keep numbers. I usually only keep what I can carry or to fund other endeavors. But, there was a time when a friend of mine talked me into publishing a book of some of my adventures. I took a few items from the journal that I always carry with me and had them made into a book; which, I'd sell from town to town.

It made me feel legit, for a while. My books sold like hotcakes at art shows and shops, but the prime place to sell them was in a large Amazonian community called Amazon Prime. For some reason, this female village of warriors just loved to read about my exploits. One of the unique features of selling to these Amazon's was their web site. A large spider built a web in the middle of town, and you could stick one of your items up on the web for everyone to see.

My book became quite popular there, so I started hanging around the web and signing books for all my Amazon customers. They would show it to all their friends and this was starting to draw more attention than I thought it ever would. One day, as I was there putting my book on the web, I was spotted by a goon who worked for the tax collector in Daggerfoot. The official's name was Abacus Finagler, a little bald gnome who worked for years for Gaspenfall's king.

He caught wind of my success and immediately grabbed a posse of his goons and rode out to bring me in. One of his henchmen was a ranger, so they tracked me down to a nearby cave I was holed up in on the outskirts of Daggersfoot. There was no way out, except for the front, and the pompous gnome knew it. I had heard rumors that Abacus enjoyed it when people wouldn't pay, because he was given full authority from the King of Gaspenfall to remedy any non-payment situation by any means necessary. Abacus stood outside the cave yelling for me to come out while his men slung a noose over a nearby tree branch.

"Give it up, Gwai Lo!" the little gnome chuckled. "You're friend Aggression, turned on you. Now, will you stick your neck out for him?!"

The posse all laughed at the joke, but I didn't find it particularly funny. I paced back and forth in the cave, biding my time. "C'mon Rogue, you're my last collection of the day, and we need to get all this gold back to the king!" Abacus yelled out while checking his sundial. "The sun's going down, and it's only a short drop, I promise it will be quick!"

I stepped out into the mouth of the cave and looked Abacus in the eye. He was only about twenty feet away, and he back peddled a bit, in surprise of my boldness. "Thanks for giving me the time," I answered. "I'm sorry I kept you waiting."

Abacus grinned back at me. "Arrest this man!" he yelled, as he turned his head.

The smile left his face, once he saw all of his guards lying on the ground with only the shadowy figure of Aggression standing over them. Aggression gave a "come here" motion with his finger, and I swear I heard some unpleasant noises coming from the little gnome. The smell confirmed my suspicion, as I approached from behind and pushed him towards the tree.

"The king is going to have both your heads for this!" cried the little gnome. "That's his gold you're stealing!"

"He can always write it off," Aggression laughed, as he tightened the noose around Abacus's neck.

We stood him up on one of his guardsman's horses as the noose was just high enough to keep him on his tiptoes. "I hope this isn't a nervous horse," I said as I jumped onto another one. "I'd hate to see him run off and leave you hanging!"

Aggression climbed and took the reins of the tax collector's wagon. "Good plan," he said to me, with a grin.

"I agree," I responded, placing a hand on my journal. "I think it may even be book worthy!"

Entry 93

I had heard rumors of a haunted road on the way to the old abandoned bell tower in the Province of Sunkensod. This seemed strange to me, because I have traveled down that road many times on my way to Robinsblind just outside of Two Snakes Lake. There was many a night where I'd sit in the Tootwhistle Tavern listening to tale after tale of this ghostly figure that would appear periodically and scare many people before taking their valuables.

The old abandoned bell tower was one of my secret hideouts when I was on the run, so I knew it quite well. I decided to look for this haunted figure by going down the road at night to see if it would appear. I bought some supplies and headed out for the bell tower. It was nightfall by the time I arrived. There were a couple of drigs squatting there that I had to shoo away, but after that, I was good to go.

I unloaded my gear and some foodstuffs into a secret room that I had discovered there, then closed the door, as I left. The night had a bit of a chill, so I wrapped my cloak around me to maintain some heat. I'd walk the road up and down, up and down, but there were no ghosts, no scary sounds; just moonlit shadows and the sound of leaves crunching under my boots. Nothing spooky to report, that's for sure. If this ghost had collected a bunch of treasure, I'm sure I would sniff it out and take it for myself!

It was in the wee late hours when I heard a wagon approaching at a slow pace. "This is no ghost," I thought to myself. Probably some rich fool on his way to Robinsblind for supplies.

I decided to give it a quick rob and then get back to watching for the ghost. When I jumped down in front of the driver, he grew wide-eyed and immediately passed out. When the passenger saw me with my black cloak blowing around, draped only in moonlight, he passed out too. "That was easy," I said to myself, as I collected most of their coins. A good thief always leaves a few for the victim. Helps them not to decide on the gallows, if you ever get caught.

For a week, it was the same routine. Wait for the ghost, get bored, rob someone. Wait for the ghost, get bored...you get my drift. I headed back to Robinsblind and sat in the tavern, eating a hot stew and listening to local scuttlebutt. I think this ghost is an urban legend or some myth the yokels just stammer on about to be cool. Because, according to them, the ghost had appeared every night that week and robbed them of their treasures.

How could that be? I was on the road every night and I didn't see anything! I would have called them out on their lie, but a bunch of their faces looked familiar to me, so I just let it go.

Entry 94

I had just held up a peace ambassador from Farlong, who was one his way to the darkest corner of Darkmist and I hit the jackpot. Not only did this tied up fool have negotiating gold, but he had a Golden Dream Ticket, as well! While I walked away from him and his knocked out patrol, he cursed at me and offered the usual victim's threats. I jumped on one of his horses and made toward Farlong, Dream Ticket in hand.

These tickets are a big deal in the Unremembered Realms; they give you access to the most wonderful place in all of Farlong, the Isle of Fortune. This island is just off the west coast of Farlong and on it is one of the most enjoyable attractions for any living soul, the Loaferlounge.

The Loaferlounge was run by a unique type of wizard, known as a Dreamwelder. These are wizards who can "patch" or "weld" you into another person's dreams. They use their special magic to build an ethereal dream cloud on another plane of existence. When you sleep, they transfer your sleeping mind to this cloud where you interact with other dreamers. The elite love it there, because inside this "dream cloud," they can be anything they want to be. It becomes an addiction for these fools, and they'll do anything to stay "connected." I guess it beats the humdrum lives that they lead back at their posh mansions.

I caught the first boat I could over to the island and was walking around enjoying the ambiance of the beautiful community. A patrol guard or two would try to shake me down, but I would just whip out my Golden Dream Ticket and they would apologetically back off, without a further word.

I had a nice lunch in a place called The Upper Crust; which I found odd; the plate had apparently been washed before they put new food on it! Talk about class! I flagged down a rickshaw and had the young man take me to the Loaferlounge. It was time to get down to business.

Once they let me through the door, I cut away from the Dreamwelding lounge and made straight for the waiting room. You see, dear reader, I couldn't care less about hobnobbing with the half-wits uploading their brains to some magic cloud. I wanted to rub elbows with their servants; the ones who hauled, prepped, or oversaw the travel, bringing their rich masters to this place.

Being a thief in the Unremembered Realms is not an easy job. There is a fine line between a household thief and a rich, happy rogue. I consider myself aimed toward the latter. I was not here to relax at all, but to collect information and gather some resources.

After a few hours of card playing and camaraderie, I got to know a few of the servants. I would lose a few games and listen to the gripes of these hard working stiffs, who would often share little details about where they live, when they sleep, and where the master has them store their loot. Some of them even figured out what I was doing and agreed to let me in their mansions, if I would kick back a gem or two for them. Some were more reluctant to share the details of their master's riches, but then, who could blame them? I didn't want to leave without discovering all of their secrets, though.

Eventually, I left the island and went on a weeklong robbing spree, visiting the mansions at night, pocketing all the wonderments of these elite snobs. Sometimes, their servants would help carry out some of these deeds. I even robbed the places where I had no knowledge of the treasure, and I never got caught once. It was a real dream come true.

That's when it hit me. I was Dreamwelding. Apparently, I never left the island after meeting with the servants. I wanted more information, so I decided to hook myself up. In my Dreamweld state, I connected with the timid servants masters and tricked them into telling me everything. People put too much trust in their dreams, and not enough into appreciating the wonderful things you can achieve in the real world.

As I woke up from the Dreamweld, I sat up in my lounge chair. A servant girl handed me a cold glass of water and helped me up. "Did you enjoy your dream," she asked.

I looked around the room and looked at the dozens of wealthy men and women still locked into their dream state. I smiled back at the girl and replied, "The best dreams are the ones that you make happen!"

Within a week, they were.

Entry 95

I was sitting in the Glutton Spoon Tavern, playing cards with the locals, when my two not-so-trusty Crimson Guild brothers, Apichat and Onquay, came sauntering in. They noticed me right away, walked over, and stood on either side of me. "You shouldn't play with him," Onquay told the other card players. "He's a cheater."

Apichat just nodded and spat. The locals slowly got up and left the game, taking their coins with them. "Thanks a lot," I spoke, while laying down my cards. "Now you two will have to pay for my lunch."

Onquay bent down to my level and looked me in the eye. "I don't think so, brother," he said, while shoving my cards onto the floor. "It's you who owes us money."

"Fools and their money are soon departed," I said, while leaning back in my chair. "But I'll tell you what. I will play you for it double or nothing."

Apichat walked around the table and pulled a chair, then sat down – never taking his eyes off mine. "It's a deal," he said, with a grin.

Onquay frowned at Apichat; his stained teeth showing, as he tried to talk his fellow thug out of it. "All we have is Elfalfuh's gold, Apichat," he warned. "If we lose it, he'll nail our tongues to the wall!"

Apichat just laughed. "Don't worry about it. Elfalfuh may be enormous and insane, but I have my wits," he replied. "I was the best card player in the Guild, and I won't let this lowlife use his sneaky cheating cards."

With that said, Apichat reached across the table with his hand out. I removed a deck of cards from my cloak and gave them to him "It's going be a fair game, you see," he motioned to the Tavernkeep. "Hey, bring me a pack of fresh cards!"

I took out my sack of coins and Onquay did the same, as he sat down between his associate and I. The Tavernkeep came over and laid a new deck on the table. Onquay started to reach for them, then he paused. "Wait a minute," he said. "What if our tricky friend here has paid him to supply fresh cheating cards!"

Apichat leaned forward and pulled out his dagger, which he held up for the Tavernkeep to see. "I reckon he's probably right," he pointed the knife at me next. "What if this snake is giving you kickbacks from all the winnings?"

I just held my hands up and smiled. "I'm your Guild brother, Appy," I replied. "Would I do such a thing?"

Onquay quickly stood up and nearly knocked over the table. "We should kill you now, worm!"

Just as there was about to be a ruckus, a local constable came through the door and yelled "There's not going to be any fight in here, boys," he spoke, while unsheathing his sword. "I'd hate to see you end up on the wrong end of justice. You get my point?!" I guess he named his sword, too!

He held the point of his sword up in my face, then slowly moved it to the other two. We all nodded and watched him lower the sword and pull a deck of cards from his pocket. "Here," he said, tossing the cards on the table. "Keep it clean."

The constable went over to a far corner of the tavern and waved for food service. I grabbed the cards and started shuffling. The other two grinned at me, "Fair and square," Apichat said, menacingly.

Within two rounds of cards, I had not only won all their money, but all their gear and most of their clothes. They were not too happy about it and made some references about me that I won't repeat in this journal. "Thank you, brothers," I said, as I stood from the table, pocketing their gold and grabbing their gear and clothing. "Tavernkeep, sell this gear for me and burn these clothes. Nobody would want to wear these flea infested rags!"

"You're going to pay for this, brother!" they said in unison, as I stepped back up to the table.

"Elfalfuh is going to get every coin back, or he'll take it out on your hide!" Onquay hissed.

I tossed a few coins on the table and said, "Here, buy yourselves some decent clothes and some tongue studs. I think you're going to need them!"

As they started yelling at each other and pointing the blame, I strolled over to the constable's table and set a stack of coins in front of him. "Thanks for bringing my cards back, Chief," I told him, while putting the deck in my pocket.

The constable just smiled and gave me a wink. "No problem," he replied. "They helped me win a few coins off my men."

I was long gone before Apichat and Onquay came to the realization that the Tavernkeep wasn't the only one in town who could be paid off. Why else would a lawman show up out of the blue with a deck of cards? In a way, Apichat was right; he was the best card man in the guild. But today, I was the best gambler.

Entry 96

I had a giant problem. I was captured by a fog giant named Zham Leaf and was being used as bait to fish for small dragons. Zham Leaf loved to eat dragons. He talked endlessly about ways to prepare them. The giant tied a rope around me, then tied the other end around a tree log. Without hardly any effort, he lowered me over the side of the Binsfjord Mountains. I have to admit, it was quite a view. The foliage in the Province of Eaglespaw was beautiful during this time of year.

I wouldn't have minded the whole incident, but he was trying to get a dragon to swallow me whole. He is what we call a Fog Giant. It's a species of giants that create their own fog, and it's not magical. They are known throughout all of the Realm of Cloverose for their large appetites and weak bellies. It's not a pleasant situation at all!

Earlier that day, I had shadowed my way through the endless caves of the mountain, so as not to disturb the short-tempered clan of dwarves, known as the Binsfjord's. I was hoping to get a close look at their most cherished magic item: the gold divining Binsfjord Spike. This spike was a miners dream! It was violently magnetic when detecting gold. It would shake loose from your hands and embed itself in rock if it detected the precious metal within it.

I managed to find where they kept it – a heavily trapped chamber, smack in the middle of the mountain. I had to dismantle two deadly traps and then pick at least three different locks on its storage case, so that I could take the spike and test out how well it fit into my backpack. I was halfway out of the mines when the magical spike started letting off a whistling sound as it detected gold.

The sound got louder and louder and I could feel it trying to move toward some undiscovered bit of gold. I heard stirrings from the dwarves, then yelling, then alarm klaxons started blaring. It was dark in the tunnels, but thanks to my lich eye, I didn't need a torch. I managed to move quickly through the mines to a small cavern with an exit. I quickly hid my pack behind a stack of rocks and crept out onto a foggy, odorous ledge, where I discovered Zham Leaf doing a bit of morning fishing.

He had already caught a small green dragon; which, was lying dead beside him. "What a bit of luck!" he exclaimed, as he picked me up and started grabbing some rope. "Dwarves make such horrible bait!"

"Thanks for not eating me," I gasped, as he squeezed me tightly in his hand. "Any bites?"

"Of course," he smiled, showing off a mouthful of gold teeth, while patting the green dragon's corpse. "I snagged this one using another thief I caught earlier!"

I looked over at the dead dragon youngling and saw a dwarven sized boot sticking out of its mouth. Zham Leaf noticed my frown and laughed, before lowering me over the side. "Don't forget to squirm! It attracts them much faster!"

I was dangling about seventy feet below the giant and could barely see him through the fog that he'd emit. I was hoping I could swing myself over to the cliff wall; my magic Spider Climbing ring could help me out of this situation. I was trying to untie myself from the ropes when I heard the screeches of a couple of baby blue dragons a hundred or so feet below me. "Bluegilds!" Zham Leaf shouted down. "Those are good eats! Wiggle around more!"

I was trying to be as still and quiet as possible, but I yelled out as an arrow jammed itself into my leg. I couldn't grab it, because my arms were tied up. That's when I noticed the small thin rope tied to the arrow. It became taught, as it started pulling me more toward the side of the cliff. As blood spurted from my leg, I heard the screeching of the blue dragons get louder. Zham Leaf must have too, because he started jiggling the line making my arrow pain even worse.

Through the fog mist, I could see two dwarves on the other end of the rope, pulling me toward the cliff by a small cave entrance. Once they got me on the ledge, they cut the rope and pulled me into the cave. "Give us our spike, thief!" they demanded, while lifting their battlehammers. "and we won't let you die slowly."

I knew these two dwarves; their names were Underhill and Vila. They were at the tavern that I was staying at a few days prior. The two had been bragging to a couple of dwarven females about the magical spike and how they can use it anytime they want. Neither of the fools had any idea I was listening, but I'm pretty sure, as they stood here, now recognizing me, they realized the foolishness of their boasting ways.

I told them I'd yell for their clan to hear and tell them of their fellow dwarves' bad judgment. I also explained where the spike was and that I could take them to it. Underhill and Vila agreed, but I think Vila still wanted to smash me. Underhill untied me, and I led them quietly up to the small cavern that was just behind Zham Leaf's fishing perch. We could hear the giant outside the entrance yelling down at some dragons, "Bring back my worm, you wyrms!"

Vila ran over and grabbed my pack from behind the rocks. He lifted it above his head and whispered softly, "Here it is!"

As he spoke, the spike fell from the pack and hit the ground. It made a loud clang, sending echoes throughout the cavern. Suddenly, it grew silent. Underhill gave Vila a stern look and was about to say something, but all of a sudden the mouth of the cavern exploded as Zham Leaf smashed through some rock, so he could fit in.

The veins in his bald head were pulsing and his golden teeth gleamed brightly, as he smiled at his good fortune. That's also when the magical spike flew from the ground and hurled itself into the golden teeth of Zham Leaf, smashing them all out!

The Fog Giant let out a huge burst of fog and ran screaming out of the cave. As the three of us stood there waving away the stench, we saw the spike lying on the cave entrance floor, surrounded by the three teeth of the giant.

Underhill looked at Vila, and they took a moment to whisper to each other in their dwarven tongue. "We realize the mistake we made boasting to our lady friends," Underhill stated. "We can't blame you for being inquisitive. Take a small tooth and beat it! Today is your lucky day."

Vila nodded in agreement, as he walked up and pulled the arrow from my leg. "And don't run off with my lucky arrow!"

They both grabbed the remaining teeth and grabbed the Binfjord Spike, before walking off into one of the tunnels leading into the cave. I tore off a piece of my tunic and wrapped up my throbbing leg. I hobbled over and collected the rest of my gear. It was a long climb back down, but I made it with not a dragon in sight.

When I got to the ground, I pulled out the gold tooth and held it up to let it gleam in the sunlight. It was not a bad day for fishing, after all.

Entry 97

Have you ever played Smash the Bottle? It's a hit in my book. I was stuck below deck on a ship with my party, as we traveled from Dragonshelm to an island off the west coast, called Alimonia. We got hired by the Mayor of Doombliss, a pompous little man with greasy hair and a collection of moles on his face that would make a farmer set traps. He hired us to deliver a letter to his beautiful ex-wife. Apparently, she left his sorry derriere and took him for half, then converted their island getaway into an assassins training camp for female orcs, ogres, ettins, butterflies, and any other bane of humanity. I don't know for sure, but I think she wanted to protect herself from his powerful friends.

"I had a wizard put a charm spell on it," he beamed, while handing me the rolled up letter. "Whoever reads this will fall madly in love with me forever!"

My party agreed to take the job and headed toward a small fishing community to hire a boat that could ferry us over to Alimonia Island. We paid for a small frigate and headed out as quickly as possible. There wasn't much room on the ship, so we had to travel below deck in one of the cramped storage areas. It wasn't long before we become bored, seasick, and a bit cranky.

To defeat our battle with tedium, Froghat the Wizard pulled a small bottle from his robe and laid it on the floor between us. "Anyone ever play spin the bottle?" he asked. "It's a secret telling game."

We all shook our heads and listened, as he explained. It was hard to take this old elf seriously, because of his Familiar, a frog he named Ozone, sat on top of his head most of the time. Dogchauw, our half-gnoll fighter, was scratching at his fleas and not even paying attention. There was a useless ranger in the group, named Stretch Markus, whose only real ability was to track the nearest buffet. And, lastly, with us was a halfling cleric, named Pickenfling. He was a disgusting little creature with a fetish for big noses. "I dig them," he'd say.

"Why would I want to share anything with this group?" I asked. "Over a child's game? What next, write a book revealing all my secrets? You people are insane!"

I turned away and tried to sleep, but the group kept spinning the bottle and telling secrets about their lives that I did not want to know and now that I did, I wished I hadn't. If it weren't for the rich mayor, I would have dumped these drig dropouts a long time ago.

Froghat revealed his failures as a cracked window salesman in Dirtspill before turning to magic. Dogchauw told of how he got beaten with rolled up papers for ruining the stock at his hometown news stand. It was hard to understand what Stretch Markus was confessing, because he was consuming a large bucket of lard that he found. The little halfling couldn't wait to tell his secrets, and the minute he did, I plugged my ears.

After a few hours of this, I stood up, walked over, and smashed the bottle under my boot! Froghat yelled "No!" but it was already too late. "That was a bottle of magical acid!"

A huge hole ate through the floor and soon the ship was taking on water at an alarming rate. Within the next five hours, I found myself floating to the island shore on a piece of debris. That ship went down faster than a dirty sock at a bogwizard's laundry shop! Oh well, at least I still had the rolled up letter and ditched the rest of the party. I believed I could do the job all by myself anyway. Fewer people to split the reward with, I figured.

As I crawled onto the sand of the beach, I must have passed out for a minute or two, because I felt two large hands pick me up off the ground and hold me up in the air. I was staring face-to-face with the ugliest ogress that I think I had ever seen. Her shallow eyes were caked in dried sleep, her nose was huge and ran freely, completely unwiped, and her breath reeked of manticore dung.

"Aren't you a handsome one!" she bellowed out in a common

tongue that I could understand. "Isn't he cute, ladies?"

Standing around her on the beach was a dozen or so gross females creatures. They all giggled and surrounded me, poking me with their claws, and some started applying some red berry paste to their lips. "He's mine!" the large ogress yelled, "He belongs to Grotessica now, so back off!"

Grotessica gave me a big hug; I thought I felt a rib crack under the pressure. That's when the letter fell from my cloak and landed at her feet. "What's this?" she asked, while setting me down to pick it up.

At this point, I didn't care about the gold any longer, I just didn't want to be this big smelly lump's boyfriend. "It's a poem I wrote for you, sweetums..." I managed to wheeze out. "Go ahead, read it and share it with your girls!"

I plugged my ears, as she read the magically charmed letter aloud to all her friends. They all stood quietly for a moment, and I swear you could see little twinkles light up in their eyes. "To Doombliss!" they all cheered simultaneously. "For love!"

They ran down the beach at quite a pace and all jumped into a large rowing vessel. I could barely keep up. During the run, I noticed Pickenfling appear out of nowhere, "Who are these ladies?" he asked me, while raising his eyebrows and grinning. I just shook my head in disgust.

"Do you ladies mind if we tag along?" he boldly asked Grotessica.

"Hop in, boys. We've got a date with the Mayor!" she replied.

Unfortunately, along the way, we found the rest of my party hanging onto Stretch Markus, who was surprisingly buoyant. I don't know how they managed to survive, but the women pulled them all aboard. We got back to the mainland fairly quickly. Grostessica's huge muscles strained with each pull of the paddle. I swear there were moments when the boat hardly touched the water. She was in love and very determined to find her new mate.

I would like to say that I hung out for the whole trip and saw the Mayor's reaction when the ogress arrived, but I didn't. Rumor has it, things got ugly, and there were multiple weddings. I don't know which of the group married Pickenfling, but I felt sorry for her.

Entry 98

I was in the city of Watercliff when a local Captain of the Guard approached my friend, Healy the Cleric, with a job offer. It seemed that a small army of goblins had decided to occupy an abandoned underground dungeon just east of the city. He told us about how they were stealing local farmers and their families for slave labor and possible food.

Healy, being a softy, agreed to take the job. The captain gave us five of his best red tunic guards and we also picked up a barbarian lady, named Helga Von Thunderskull. She was large, muscular, and nearly as tall as a half-ogre. She grunted more than she talked and wore only tanned goblin skin for armor. The hammer she carried was crafted from some magical stone; I swear you could see a face print mashed in it, if you looked hard enough.

After getting briefed about the mission, we left for the dungeon. Healy was excited about rescuing the families and restoring peace to the area, while I was more interested in saving the gold from the greasy claws of the goblin horde.

Soon we were knee deep in battle within the dungeon. The red tunics lasted for a bit, but had gotten killed off one-by-one. I'm glad I didn't get to know them personally, or I might have cared when they snuffed it. I was not surprised at the fighting prowess of Helga. She rapped on the goblins skulls with her hammer, like she was playing an assortment of blood filled drums. Brains, eyes, and teeth would shoot in every direction. There was one that she hit so hard, that its ears stayed in place for a moment as the hammer smashed the rest of goblins head deep into its chest.

Another fun moment happened when Healy wasn't looking, and a goblin eye flew into his mouth. I asked him if having a new pupil left a foul taste in his mouth. He didn't laugh.

Down around the fifth level, we encountered a horde so large, that we ended up hiding in a small room that I found behind a secret door. Even Helga had the common sense to duck away with us, though she was eager for more blood. We were sitting there going over our options when I noticed iron pipes that laced the ceiling in this room. Healy lifted me up, and I studied the pipes, while Helga impatiently paced the floor.

"I don't care if I die," she grunted, while taking a moment to sniff her armpit. "Let's kill more goblins! Waiting here stinks!"

"She's right, Healy," I said, while climbing down. "It does stink. Some of these are sewer drains coming down from the upper levels. "They must run off to somewhere."

"So?" Healy stated. "Are you suggesting we abandon the families and flush ourselves out?"

"I'll never run!" Helga's voice rose. "My hammer craves brains!"

"Calm down, you two. See those other set of pipes over there?" I pointed to the opposite side of the room where more pipes were. "That's fresh water coming up from some spring. Why don't we re-arrange the pipes? Let's turn this party into a foul ball!"

Healy shook his head in disgust, but the female barbarian grinned from ear to ear. We spent the next hour rearranging the pipes. It was just in time, too. We heard lunch bells ringing. We waited and waited as the goblins came down the hallway toward a dining area that, apparently, we had been hiding behind. Slowly, but steadily, the goblin army started walking out of the room and caressing their bellies. "That soup was awful." I heard one complain. "Tell the chef his food was crappy today."

Within an hour, the hallways were lined with goblins throwing up and clutching their stomachs. Healy and I ran through the rest of the dungeon collecting the farmer's families and setting them free. Once in a while, I'd find a chief and rescue the gold, and occasionally, a gem from them. There wasn't much resistance.

As we guided the families out, a huge goblin war chief crawled up to us and sputtered. "Our food...poisoned by you!"

"Actually," I replied. "It was the higher ups. They dropped their orders, from their bowl to yours!"

Healy did chuckle at this joke, before we stepped over the war chief on our way out. Then, we noticed the barbarian was not following us. "You coming?" I asked her.

She just smiled and raised her hammer. "My hammer is still hungry; it's craving just desserts!"

Healy almost laughed at the joke, but he remembered the flying goblin eye. So he clamped his mouth shut, as we left the dungeon dancing to the rhythmic tune of Helga Von Thunderskull's pounding hammer.

Entry 99

If you are in the Unremembered Realms when it's dark, there's a chance you'll run into one of the RedEye Knights. They are a noble order of paladins who guard the realm folks from sunset to sunrise. They earned the nickname of RedEye, because of their working hours, their bloodshot eyes, and their addiction to coffee.

If you had a bugbear on your tail at three o'clock in the morning, it was possible you could be safe by leading him into a local Java grind, where the RedEyes would hang out. Monsters didn't last too long fighting these battle hardened paladins. They were usually fully armored and carried a light saber in each hand. A RedEye once let me hold one and I was shocked by how lightweight it was. The metal was stronger than a heavier saber. You didn't have to be a pocket alchemist to figure out these weapons were magically enhanced.

The RedEye Knights owed me a favor, because I helped them during one of their darkest moments, the era of Asmatticus. Word in the realms had been that a RedEye Knight got sick of the all-nighters, and his sleep deprivation had turned him against the RedEye Temple. His name was Asmatticus, and he was building up his forces, so he could eliminate the RedEye Order, once and for all!

The RedEye's caught wind of his plot to build a temple of his own. Asmatticus planned to fill it with armies of undead, who would never be subject to the tiredness of sleep. This Undeath Temple was to be the new shining star of Darkenbleak, so the RedEyes were hiring rogues to silently infiltrate their current headquarters.

Apparently, Asmatticus had paid a one-thousand-year-old lich, named Coffinhack, for the plans to make this all happen. Rumor had it, that this powerful lich spent over 500 years, endless supplies of gold, and even stole the life forces of his followers to make the magical scroll, which held the plans and the magic to make the Temple happen. I guess they were only a few spell components away from a making this a reality.

So, the RedEyes launched their rogue force to attack the unfinished temple, hoping to slip one of us in to steal the plans for this new building. While others were caught up in the hand-to-hand battles, I found a way to slip into the fortress and keep myself firmly hid in the shadows.

Freshly raised undead by the dozens were going up and down the hallways, along with some orcs and a few kobolds. I searched through the corridors for what seemed like an hour, before I stopped by a doorway, because I heard the laborious breathing of what could only be that of Asmatticus. Just as I put my hand on the door handle, I spotted an open door across the hallway. It was a well-lit room, empty of creatures, with a large table, some chairs, and a small scroll that sat unrolled on top.

I slipped into the room, saw that it was the exact magical scroll I was looking for, and grabbed it. I rolled it up and stuck it in one of the secret pockets of my cloak. That's when I heard the clacking footsteps of the lich king. I didn't know what to do, so I ran to the other door across the hallway and opened it, before slipping inside. I immediately regretted the decision, because the odor was tremendous!

Asmatticus was inside this bathroom, using one of the stalls and making some of the most horrible sounds. He would breathe deeply, catch his breath, and let out a sigh. I didn't know what to do, but I heard some yelling from outside in the hallway, so I hid in the stall next to ex-RedEye. "Too much coffee?" I asked, as he let out another round of horrifying sounds.

"It's a RedEye Knight's curse!" yelled out the angry man, between groans. "Soon, I'll have my revenge!"

A couple of guards came in, but Asmatticus yelled at them through the stall door until they left. "Oh no," he groaned. "Nobody replaced the cleaning paper! Just my luck!"

He tapped on the wall of the stall between us. "Excuse me, buddy. Can you help a fellow out?"

I almost started to panic. I didn't see any on my side either. When I bent down to look and see if any had rolled off the tumbler, the scroll fell out of my cloak and landed on the floor, rolled under the wall, and into the former paladin's stall. His hand snagged it up right away. "Thanks, man!" Asmatticus chimed.

I heard the paper rustling around a bit, then a crumple. Next, I heard Asmatticus stand up and wash his hands in the basin. "Thanks, buddy," was all he said, as he left the room whistling.

Needless to say, I made my way out of the temple and back to the RedEye Knights, where I explained everything. "Another well-made plan down the hole!" the leader laughed. "I just hope that lich doesn't realize what happened to his un-life's work!"

I never heard anything about Asmatticus again, nor was the Un-death Temple ever completed. I always wondered if Coffinhack ever caught on to what happened. If he did, I'm sure Asmatticus, just like the Lich's scroll, was flushed out of existence.

Entry 100

Back when I was a kid, I used to dream of time travel. Not because I cared about the future; I figured that would take care of itself. I mostly wanted to go back to the past. Mostly, because I wanted to track down the shadowy thief who stole my one-of-a-kind magically enhanced super sucker that I had purchased at my favorite local candy shop. I had saved for this treat for over a year!

The day I bought this wonder lolly, I walked out of the store with my mother and this thief in a dark cloak ran by and grabbed my one of a kind candy. I had always figured I'd never know the rotten scoundrel's name, but I finally got a chance to travel back to that very day, thanks to Aloonda the Sorceress, who owed me a favor. "Are you sure you want to do this?" she asked.

I gave the thumbs up, and she opened a time portal right in front of me. "Hurry, rogue. I can't hold this open long."

I did not hesitate. As I stepped through, I noticed the city surroundings; how the buildings looked so hauntingly familiar. I was a bit disorientated and stumbled around for a moment. That's when I saw it, some blonde haired kid holding a rare sucker that looked just like mine. Knowing I had only minutes to spare, I ran up in front of the candy store, snatched the candy from the kid and ran back through the portal.

"Did you find out anything," Aloonda asked.

"Regretfully, no," I responded, "but I got the candy I've waited for my whole life!"

Entry 101

It was a sad day. I was attending the funeral of a fighter, named Fodderman. He was a good guy, but the young warrior did not seem to be cut out for the business of adventuring. Fodderman joined up with my party when, our fighter, YaMacha Derschingler, called in sick, because of a runny nose. We were supposed to raid the temple of some moon worshipping cult that had sprung up in the Tanglewood Forest.

A couple of days before, my party had been at the temple, ready to fight. Bok and Choy, the archer ninjas, put well-placed arrows into the lungs of the guards when we approached the back door to this dingy foul place. I dismantled a few of the traps and Healy the Cleric shooed away a couple of zombies, before we set foot inside. Fodderman was feeling confident and motioned us back from the big wooden door. "I want to be a hero. Let this be the first step in my journey to make a difference!" That's when he tripped on the Not Welcome mat. Poor Fodderman did a face plant on the hard marble floor in front of a small marble statue. It wobbled, momentarily, before falling on top of him, crushing his skull.

"Can you heal that?" I asked Healy, as I pointed to the fighters crushed head.

"Not really," he said, popping one of the eyes back in.

We had a team meeting and decided to drag this unlucky sap back to his family. We figured it was now best to wait until Ya-Macha got over his malady. The situation was irritating, because we were all itching to wipe out this new cult. These weird cultists had popped up out of nowhere, like a bad swamp rash. The big rumor

138

was that the leader was a smooth talking cleric; a real charmer with a soothing demeanor.

While at Fodderman's funeral service, I left the finger food table and wandered over to the fallen warrior's casket. Digby, the Funeral Director, came over and shook my hand. "He was a good man," he whispered, softly. "With great potential!"

"I agree," I replied, as I slipped Digby's gold ring off his finger, without his knowledge. "Such a brave fighter."

Digby was a pleasant fellow. I almost felt sorry for taking his ring. After exchanging a few pleasantries, I excused myself for some fresh air. I slipped his ring on my finger as a reminder to sell it at the next flip-n-wink I came across. It didn't appear to be magical; it was just gold with a lightning bolt over a moon. It wasn't long before I gathered with the rest of my party outside when YaMacha showed up. He was looking better and was even smiling. "Let's go to the temple tomorrow," he said, with a twinkle in his eye, "...and slice this cult in half."

The next day, when the sun came up and the morning's mist cleared, we made our way through the Tanglewood forest toward the temple. YaMacha was finally over his sniffles, so I was feeling a bit more confident about our chance of survival. As we neared the temple, YaMacha decided that a front door approach would be faster than sneaking in the back again. So, he tiptoed up to the new guards and daintily picked them both up by their necks. YaMacha squeezed their throats until their tongues popped out and chucked them into a pile. Then, he approached the big double doors. Both were embossed with a lightning bolt over a moon symbol, just like on my ring.

He gently popped open the doors with his war boots, whilst loudly screaming his war cry. Unlike Fodderman, YaMacha grabbed the Not Welcome mat and rammed it into the cake hole of a defending guard. Bok and Choy were dropping guards left and right, while Healy was dispatching a small group of undead that was pouring into the large pillared chamber that we had entered. I was just about to flank some guards, when a zombie caught me by the arm and nearly bit into me. I had turned just right, so he missed and his teeth sunk into my small backpack.

When I whirled around to stab him with Magurk, I paused, realizing I was standing face-to-face with Fodderman. His head was shoddily reconstructed and there was some stuff missing, but it was Fodderman, alright. I would even say that he may have looked pretty good, considering he was kind of an ugly bloke. I was just about to stab him, when I saw a toe tag. So, I maneuvered him over to a stack of long wooden crates and used Magurk to impale him to them.

I bent down and read the toe tag, "Property of Digby's Funeral Parlor."

That's when I figured it out. The long crates were caskets! So, this is where the temple was getting its fresh supply of zombies. I looked at the lightning bolt ring I had on my hand and remembered the carvings on the front door. "Hold on!" I screamed, while holding up the ring. "We're here to join!"

With that said, the battle halted. When the guards and undead saw the ring, they ceased. My party, a bit surprised, followed my lead. Moments later, fifteen dark robed clerics appeared out of nowhere and surrounded us all. "So you've come to join our crusade," a phlegmy voice asked. "Do you wish to reach for the stars, to modify your vehicles, and to ride the moon as lightning!?"

A starry-eyed cleric dressed in polished leather armor came out from behind a pillar. Engraved in the armor was the moon with a lightning bolt going through it. "I don't know where you got that ring initiate, but you do not appear to be the usual volunteers and I doubt that you are here to become one with us!"

With that, all the clerics started chanting, my party gathered itself into a defensive circle as we became surrounded by clerics, guards, and undead. "I am Halestorm, the mighty priest of this cult. You will now sleep and be transformed!"

At those words, my party crumpled to the ground under some powerful sleep spell. I pretended to fall asleep as well. It's a good thing I was still wearing my non-resting amulet that made me immune to any sleep magic. The clerics all stopped chanting, as Halestorm approached me. "How did this one get a ring?" He asked one of his followers. "Look, he carries some kind of book. It looks like one of our zombies bit it."

When he reached down to grab this very journal, I quickly stood up and slid behind him, putting Magurk up to his throat. "Tell your gang of lunartic's to back off."

The cleric immediately waved to his followers to obey. "Now, tell them to remove the sleep spell off my friends. Especially the big guy with the big glowing axe that's covered with blood," I stated. "He's our negotiator!"

I wish I could have let Halestorm go, at this point, because I felt some warm moistness soak through my cloak and heard the sprinkles hit the floor. The rest of my party was soon on their feet and smiling at our situation. YaMacha immediately came up to my prisoner with his big axe and was just about to kill him. "Wait!" Halestorm cried out. "I'm not a cleric; I'm a cobbler!"

His acolytes, as well as the undead horde, turned toward him in shock. "What?!" I asked. "This had better not be some joke!"

"No, no, no. I promise," Halestorm begged. "I was fixing shoes for the dead bodies. Digby thought I had an eye for detail, so he asked me if I wanted to work on a secret project with him. He's a charming guy, so I said, sure. Anything beats being a cobbler for stiffs."

"The next thing I knew, I was recruiting clerical drop-outs for this dumb cult thing and my followers were starting to grow! Digby provides me with all the recent dead I need, and that enables me to be part of a bigger army that he's planning on building," he explained. "These are just dupes for a much greater threat!"

No wonder they all stopped in their tracks when they saw Digby's ring. They thought I was working for Digby. I could tell by the look on the all the priests faces that they were not happy with what Halestorm had just confessed. "Why don't we leave these dupes with their priest," I told my party, shoving Halestorm to the ground in front of me. "I'm sure they have a lot to talk about."

Halestorm cried out, as the surviving priests and guards all angrily tore into him. As my party walked out, we decided to go after the much bigger game; Digby. It was the least we could do for poor old Fodderman. "Hold on a minute," Healy told me at the front door. "I'll be right back."

Later that night, Digby sat in his office filling out paperwork and writing some notes. He did not notice me enter the room and by the time that he did, it was already too late. I held him down, while YaMacha, with Bok and Choy, tied him to his chair. We sat listening to a confession of tears, as he explained all the secret temples he had been constructing in the area. He was even kind enough to reveal all the funding sources for his operation. Gold had been pouring in from all the provinces of the Unremembered Realms. Some from sources that shocked even me. Corruption seemed to know no bounds.

"Please, don't kill me," he begged. "I'll turn over a new leaf! I could join your party and help use what I know to save the realms!"

"We won't kill you, fool!" Bok hissed. "And we don't need you either, we've already added a new fighter to our party."

Choy stepped out of the way to reveal Fodderman the Zombie, wearing Halestorm's bloodied leather armor. "We've got him right here," Healy stated, with a giant smirk, "...and he's been dying to eat you!"

Fodderman was finally a hero. Not only did he get a fresh meal, but the undead fighter had also destroyed the head of a massive ring of corruption. You could say he unlived up to his new potential. We left that night with maps, scrolls, and plans of attack. I wore the ring that would get us all into the soon-to-be defunct cult facilities, but best of all, Fodderman was now one of us – a true hero of the realms.

✦ ⟫✦⟪ ✦

Entry 102

I was sent a priority scroll from Harbortree Retirement Village. It stated my requirement to start doubling my payments there to take care of my senile uncle, Doffcap. He had a touch of the Oltimers Malady, so he needed around-the-sundial care. I didn't mind funding the care of the old loon, but getting my fees doubled overnight just doesn't happen, without some kind of investigation being called for.

So, I headed to the southwest edge of Sunkensod, until I reached the large iron gates of the retirement community. Harbortree was a beautiful place; one that a lot of heroes looked forward to in retirement. It was mostly good weather and the view of the coast was breathtaking. The community was surrounded by a giant wall that helped to keep monsters and ill-willed people out, so the residents could live out their final days in peace.

As I approached the gates, two large, heavily armored guards blocked my entrance. "I'm here to see about this bill," I told them, as I approached, waving the scroll. "My uncle is a resident here."

The two guards looked at each other, then at me. "No one is allowed in anymore – bosses orders. Either pay the bill, or we'll chuck the old scruff into the drink," the larger of the two said, forcefully. "If you have a complaint, write a letter to Cathidar, the new Community Master."

The other guard came up to me and jammed his finger into my chest. "No one comes in or out without approval from Cathidar," he spat.

"Not a problem," I replied through clenched teeth, before turning around and walking away.

Within the next hour, I was approaching the two guards again. But, this time I had donned my magical Hat of Disguising. To the guards, I appeared to be an old man with a slight limp. "I'm done with saving the world boys," I stated. "I'm looking to retire."

The two guards surrounded me, offering me a writing quill and a clipboard stacked with papers. "Place your initials in all the marked places, Gramps. You're going to love what Harbortree offers," the big guard said in a sarcastic tone.

After signing, the two guards each grabbed me by an elbow and walked me up to the doors, which immediately opened, and they set me down on my feet, once I was inside. "Now get to work, chump!" one spouted off to me, as they both laughed and high-fived, before walking off.

Revealed before me, was what was left of the retirement resort. Located in the center of the courtyard, was a huge hole with makeshift stairwells and bamboo handicap ramps leading down into a mine shaft. Working in the mines, were hundreds of gray or white haired elderly men, most of which were looking poorly. There were humans, elves, dwarves, halflings, orcs, and an occasional aging gnoll. "Where are all the women?" I asked an aged dwarf, who was just about to carry down a couple of buckets of water.

"Cathidar has them all," he said, weakly. "For his gray harem."

"Where does he stay?" I asked.

The dwarf nodded in the direction of a lovely estate that was just past some colorful fruit trees over a small hill, to the west of the mine. "What are we mining for?"

"This area used to be the cemetery," the dwarf explained. "Until the day they hit a few chips of gold when burying a former resident, a buddy of mine named Doffcap."

I don't know if he noticed my angry frown, but he continued his explanation. "Now, the Director is obsessed with finding more gold. Every bit of money is funneled into his mining operation. We are forced to work until we die!"

"Why don't you fight back?" I asked. "Some of you used to be great adventurers!"

"We're old and malnourished," he further explained. "Plus, nobody has ever gotten by his top guard, Pummellgums."

He pointed to a large, green Mossblood Ogre who stood outside of the estate. Pummellgums looked big, very big. He wore a black spiked war helmet, blood stained leather armor, and carried a large club riddled with spikes. "Follow me, Buckets," I told the old dwarf, "I have a plan!"

The dwarf raised a white eyebrow, but didn't raise a fuss. He sat down his water and followed me to the estate where Cathidar was about to have a quick dagger-to-heart conversation with Magurk. Pummellgums hardly batted an eye when we hobbled up. "Excuse me, sir," I said, shakily. "We've discovered more gold!"

Pummellgums' dark green eyes grew large, and his grin was as wide as the space between his eyes. "Show me the gold, you old fools!" he commanded.

"Yes, sir," Buckets replied, hoping I knew what I was doing.

"I'm too tired," I huffed. "I can't make it."

Pummellgums frowned. "Get on my back, you old maggot; I'll carry you myself!"

With that said, the ogre lifted me up onto his back, so I grabbed hold of his neck. "Finally! Gold!" he said, as he started walking. "Looks like it's over for you old sods!" he laughed. "Your work here is done; it's the end of the line!"

"I couldn't agree more," I replied, pulling out Magurk. "It was nice working with you."

Moments later, I was kicking in the front door of the estate, dragging the ogre's head behind me. Lying on a couch in the center of the room, was Cathidar, being fed grapes and getting foot massages by the women of his "gray harem." They all just stood there, wide-eyed, while I removed my disguise and pointed at the fat, balding elderly man.

I turned my hand into a thumbs down and the ladies smiled and turned on Cathidar, like a pack of gray wolves. I have to admit that I've seen many things in my travels, but watching this man being drowned in his used bedpan was a definite first!

Entry 103

I used to hang out in the Dock Port Kill 'n' Grill for a while. I got to know the locals fairly well, especially an old, overweight wizard, named Veedo. He was always good for a laugh, because he would come running into the tavern blabbering on in his indecipherable way. "Faeries! My toof, gabblegoo tawa sumderby help me, hut, old beano shoe!"

I didn't know what he was saying half the time, but I decided, one day, to help the old guy. From what I had gathered, he had a small home in the Faerwood Forest (a place loaded with Faeries and tons of other magical creatures). I learned that the creatures of the forest didn't like him there siphoning their magic, so they sent a group of prankenfaeries to scare him off.

Every day, Veedo would leave and then come home to find some complicated pranking device that would hit him with a pie in the face, shave off an eyebrow, or stuff a dead fish down his socks. Veedo took me to his house and began showing me the weird collection of magical components that he'd acquired from spots in the forest. "The faeries, toom uch wult to catch," he said, "So I hira one of dem fur da spy, it's a mo goda tipe tayyyy!"

This little wood faerie flew up and landed on my hand. "My name is Glom," he giggled. "I'm Veedo's helper!"

I knew this little crud was lying straight away. "So, you understand what this magic user is saying?" I asked.

"Yeah," he replied. "It's a mix of our language and yours. He's lost between two worlds."

I hung around these two for a week and the prankenfaeries did not show up once. I figured the creatures were a little scared seeing me there, so they had given up on bothering Veedo. Glom would disappear, now and again, but he was always back to help the old wizard with some of his experiments. One morning, Glom showed up with a colorful berry from some rare plant and flew it over to Veedo, who was mixing some kind of potion in a vial.

"Come see this," the little wood faerie said. "We're finally ready to complete our potion!"

"Goom palla da!" cheered Veedo.

I walked over to his lab area and watched as he mashed the berry and sprinkled it in the vial. The second it hit the liquid, there was a huge poof that knocked me backward onto the floor. As the green smog cleared, I could hear dozens of voices laughing and cheering. It was prankenfaeries. They had been waiting to play the final gag.

As I looked around, I noticed that my world had changed. All the furniture in the house was gigantic! It slowly dawned on me that I was now the size of a wood faerie, approximately three inches tall! I could see the now diminutive Veedo in the distance being grabbed by prankenfaeries and then, flown off. "Abba gabba loonk maird!" he shouted, as they flew him out of a window.

The ones left behind started to look for me, so I ran under a stuffed chair. I was about to activate my Blending Cloak, but I felt a hand go over my mouth and pull me up into a hole in the bottom of the chair. "Be quiet," a female voice whispered. "Hide with me."

I turned around to see a beautiful female faerie with long auburn hair and dazzling green eyes. She flew over into a shadowy corner inside the chair. She put her finger to her lips and gave me the shush sign, although I already knew.

Prankenfaeries were flying and running all over the place looking for me. Glom was barking out orders, trying hard to convince his brethren that I hadn't left. "That one is as sneaky as we are," he warned. "Don't let him exit this house alive!"

When they did search inside the chair, I wrapped the female and myself in my cloak, while they flew past us. One almost had a visit with my friend Magurk, but the female stopped me. "Don't give us away," she whispered. "They are incredibly dangerous!"

After a few hours, the prankenfaeries had given up and left to mess with their new mini-wizard. I think they knew I'd be impossible to find. The female introduced herself as Amberfawn, and I have to admit, I was a little taken back by her beauty. I decided to stick around for a while. If I was going to be this small for now, I decided, she wouldn't be the worst creature to hang around.

For the next few weeks, we spent time together going out to places she thought would be fun. She showed me the nuances of the faerie world and tried to explain the unexplainable, like the missing colors of the color spectrum that my human eyes couldn't see. Much like other faeries, she tended to talk a lot, so I mostly listened, taking in every bit of knowledge that I could.

One night, she let me know where the prankenfaeries lived. They had a camp inside a rotten section of a fallen tree with a hole in the top. They had tiny little tents and probably kept Veedo tied up to a stake in between them all. I felt sorry for the old codger, he wasn't really out to hurt anybody, and these prankenfaeries were mean little twerps. Eventually, Amberfawn told me that they kept a hidden stash of treasure in the forest somewhere. From that point, I knew I had to perform a rescue...and get Veedo too.

Of course, she tried to talk me out of it. She considered her faerie brethren quite dangerous. She had grown to care for me and I was starting to feel the same for her, but settling down isn't in my nature. Also, the thought of not chasing after the treasure would eventually drive me crazy. One night, over dinner at her place, we discussed options for pulling off a rescue. She asked me for a private moment, so I went and sat on the edge of the lip of the entrance to her home, which was carved out of a large and slowing crawling Wanderoot Tree.

Amberfawn didn't realize it, but I watched her disappearing into a secret door of her home. I turned around and gazed at the stars, before she reemerged and quietly sat down next to me. Amberfawn handed me a map and a small vial.

"What's in the vial?" I asked.

"One drop of this and you'll be big again," she explained, then looked down sadly. "But, I know of no other way for you to become small again."

We looked at the countless stars for a bit, not saying much. Before parting for the night, we both agreed on our plan for a sneak attack. Amberfawn rested her head on my shoulder for a moment, before going off to sleep.

Not long after that, I climbed down to a lower branch where I had been camping out. I rested on a makeshift hammock, but couldn't sleep. I couldn't get my mind off that secret door; I made a decision to investigate. I waited for about twenty minutes, before I climbed back up and used my Blending Cloak go in, without being spotted.

When I snuck in, I peeked into her resting area, and she was not there! I immediately started to think maybe things weren't as they appeared. I went over to the secret door and pushed the nearly invisible latch to open it.

When it silently opened, I saw long rows of shelves, all lining this large section of carved out tree. Sitting on the shelves, were countless varieties of teeth; all labeled. I stood in amazement gawking at the seemingly endless collection. There were also gold and silver coins sitting on bare areas of the shelves. "So, now you know," Amberfawn spoke, as she walked in from behind me.

I turned around and looked into her bright green eyes. She looked more sad than scared. "I go around at night, exchanging teeth for money!" she explained. "I guess that makes me some kind of weirdo to you."

I just smiled and took her hand, "Actually, my dear, I think we have a lot more in common than you think."

She looked bewildered, so I continued. "I collect teeth as well, especially the gold ones!"

I explained to her my technique of tavern fighting for teeth, all to make a quick coin. "So, you're the one who's been keeping me busy!" she said, in a moment of realization. "I don't know whether to slap or hug you!"

"That's the story of my life," I explained, "...and I vote for the hug!"

She blinked a few times and shrugged. "Yeah, I'm alright with that."

We laughed for a bit while we hugged, then shared more honest stories about our lives. It was nice just being able to talk for a change. Eventually, the talk made its way back to our rescue plan and we decided to go ahead with it at that very moment.

Amberfawn watched, as I grabbed an arrow and removed the tip. Then, I swabbed the end with some of the enlargement potion. When I was ready, Amberfawn picked me up and flew me through the woods in the direction of the prankenfaerie camp. When we got to the old log, I could see all the tents below us. The sun was just starting to blink over the horizon, so I knew we had to hurry. I spotted Veedo asleep on the ground in between all the tents, so I took out my magical Swatfly bow and loaded the arrow.

Just as I was about to let the arrow fly, I spotted Glom the Prankenfaerie. He stepped out of his tent and rubbed his eyes. He must have heard Amberfawn's wings, because he looked up and saw me ready to shoot my arrow. His eyes grew large in disbelief. He was about to yell out something when I let the arrow go, and it nailed Veedo square in the chest. With a loud "FOOMPF!" Veedo was immediately full size again.

The large magic user's weight crushed the log and everything underneath it. Veedo sat up "Hey, what hoopend?"

As he stood up and looked around, I could see all the little stains on the back of his robe. Amberfawn flew me over to his shoulder, where I explained everything. Veedo was grateful for what we had done and asked what he could do to repay our kindness. "Can you make a potion to reshrink me?" I asked.

"Shoor do now!" he said, before explaining about the missing berry component that Glom had revealed to him. "Too bad about yoon labst treasure map!"

"It's not lost, Veedo," I said, as Amberfawn flew me down to the Glom stain on his rump. "I just have to peel it off."

Things worked out well. I split the treasure with Veedo and Amberfawn and the garbling wizard made the potion I had requested. Amberfawn and I have a great relationship, to this very day. We don't see each other often; she has her job, I have mine. But, when we do get together, we see eye-to-eye and in all the little ways appreciate our life together.

Entry 104

One of my more creative endeavors was hanging out at local taverns disguised as a hireling. My handy magical Hat of Disguising made it easy to blend in with the local slobs. When a sinister party of bandits pulled up in their horse wagon, I'd jump in the back with a couple of others. We'd ride amongst the empty crates until we reached some stronghold that these guys thought they were going to conquer.

If they didn't manage to beat the soldiers of the fort or village, I would just ride off with the horses and sell them for a few coins. If they did win, they usually came out in rough enough shape for me to beat up and tie them to a tree. "Go get our gold, fool," they'd shout, before I'd lay them flat with a right hook. I always enjoyed the look of shock on the other hireling's faces when they witnessed my boldness.

Of course, I'd take most of the gold back into the fort to its rightful owners, but I always made sure they agreed to pay my hireling pals and me a reward. One day, as I was splitting up the gold with the others, a fellow hireling told me an unusual story.

He informed me that there was a cruel warrior who had been fleecing local villages. His name was Lout Smashenbegger; I guess he took extreme pleasure in killing the defenseless. Rumor had it, that he used magic potions to "juice" himself up before conquering his victims.

It only took a couple of days travel to track Lout's whereabouts. I found he had just left the small village of Mudbudder, just to the south of Trippinfalls. The surviving villagers came out of their huts as I entered the town and told me to hide, before Lout would come back and see me. They didn't have much in Mudbudder, but what they did have, he took. "Please," said an elderly woman. "We'll pay you whatever we can. Just return what he stole."

"One gold coin," I said to the woman, "Just point me in the right direction."

She agreed, and I turned to the direction that she pointed. "I'll be back," I said, as I walked off.

I knew he was walking in the direction of the hamlet of Tagwart, so I made a guesstimate as to when he'd show up. I also knew he was weighted down with treasure, so he'd have to make a stop in the larger town of Turtlesong to bank it or buy some goods.

When I got to Turtlesong, the man at the Happy Harpy's Flip-N-Wink told me Lout had just left. He had spent his gold on a valuable ring and some potions. I turned in a superbly cut gem that I had from my hireling ruse, also in exchange for some potions, before I headed out the door.

I finally caught up to the large man on the outskirts of Tagwart. He was strong-arming a local into telling him about the village's defenses. He smacked the guy and shoved him to the ground. I put my hat on and made myself look like a half-orc. I walked out of the brush and approached Lout, carefully. "Need any help, Mister?"

Lout stopped, looked me over, and then smiled. "I don't pay much, hireling," he said. "Caddy my pack, it will be full soon."

The pack had some gear and was lined with potions. "I'm about to rob this village, if you want to tag along," Lout continued. "Don't drag your feet half-breed; throats don't cut themselves!"

I followed him to the village square. The villagers seemed to scatter at the sight of this scary man. "Send out your best warrior, then send out your gold!" he hollered. "You have five minutes, or you all die now!

He turned to me and gave a wink. I just smiled back. Within a few moments, a small, skinny farm boy came out with a rusty short sword. He was visibly shaking, yet knew someone had to step up for the honor of his village. "Are you prepared to die, farmboy?" Lout laughed.

The farmboy just stood there trying to adjust his oversized helmet, so he could see. Lout turned back to me and said, "Let's make this brutal. Hand me the Potion of Ogre Strength from my pack!"

While I fumbled in the backpack with one hand, I grabbed from my cloak a Potion of Weakness that I bought in Turtlesong and passed it to the giant man. He smiled, then bit the cork off the top and guzzled the potion. "Let the fight begin," he yelled, as he tried to pick up his sword.

That's when he realized he could barely lift it. He struggled for a moment and seemed to get more tired, as he tried. The farmboy stood there looking on, not knowing what to think. I removed my hat of disguising, so the farmboy and Lout could both see that I was no longer what I appeared to be. Lout had a look of shock, while the boy's smile grew from ear-to-ear. I motioned to Lout with my hand and humbly bowed to the farmboy.

Poor Lout went out with a whimper, as the boy quickly achieved his new position as local hero. Who knows, maybe this kid will become a great fighter someday; he just needed a little confidence.

A few days later, I returned to the Mudbudder village with what was left of their gold and the head of Lout Smashenbeggar. The senior woman approached me at the celebratory feast and tried to give me some gold.

When I pushed her hand gently back, I reached into my pocket and grabbed a coin of my own; which, I flipped over to her palm. "As I told you, one gold coin."

It was money well spent.

Entry 105

When I was a teen, I was discovered by the Crimson Roof Thieves Guild and started running messages for them. Sometimes it would be information or it might be of the ransom type. I'm not saying that's good or bad; it was not my place to make that call. Dealing with the Crimson Roof Brotherhood was not always easy, but it did pay handsomely.

For one assignment, I was sent to Lhentil Keep to deliver a message. It was for a couple of squatting Druids who had taken up residence in one on the guild's secret hideouts. They had been warned before, but they were locally infamous freeloaders with a reputation for being difficult. Flipflop and Jinglemilk would slam the door in my face, whenever I warned them to leave.

"Nobody's here!" they would shout, as I pounded on the door after hearing it lock. I tried to pick the lock, but all I would hear is laughter and pan flute music being played. "You can't pick a magic seal!" one of them would eventually chortle.

Being so young, I knew I couldn't mess with them too much; my training wasn't that far along yet. I figured I'd just wait the bums out. The outhouse was just outside, and they'd have to come out sooner or later. But, I forgot they were druids and after two days, it dawned on me – they were probably just using a pail in one of the bedrooms.

One night, when I thought they might be sleeping, I managed to loosen the bolts on a reachable window and slowly slid it open. I was relieved to see that they were crashed out in the living area, surrounded by half-eaten quiche burgers and some nutbread crusts. As I confidently lowered my foot down on the floor, I heard a squish and felt a watery sensation shoot up my leg. Flipflop and Jinglemilk roared out in laughter, as I realized they weren't asleep and were waiting for me to break in and step into their sluff bucket.

As you can probably guess, I was furious. I fell backward out of the window and into a Rashberry bush. I spent the next few hours at the local cleric's getting ointment and explaining my condition, known as "stinkfoot."

By the time I got back, I could see the two druids dancing around the apartment with a couple of female druids they must have invited over. I could hear them laughing at me. I swear, I sat outside for hours just staring at the place. I was determined to get them out of there that very night!

Just before nightfall, I noticed smoke in the kitchen and one of the druids opened a window to let it out. "Must be making more bread" I thought to myself. These kooks loved nutbread. Then, an idea hit me...and I smiled. When all things settled and the sun had given way to the moon, I peaked in the window to see the druids all passed out. All that was left was some incense; which, was just about burnt out.

I crawled through the kitchen window, reached into the vat of nut flour, and covered myself head to foot. The powder smelled nice, so I pocketed their recipe; which, had been left on the counter.

Moments later, I burst into the living room, wailing like there was no tomorrow. Flipflop, Jinglemilk, and their lady friends fell off their cushions, screaming and scrambling for the door. "Gwai Lo! Gwai Lo!" they cried, "It's a ghost, man!"

The story of how I scared them out of the hideout became something of a legend amongst the brothers of the guild and also around local areas. I was given a full membership and to this day my brothers refer to me as Gwai Lo or The Ghost Man.

Entry 106

I stood in front of the ancient, smiling red dragon in complete awe. It was a legendary creature to all who lived in the Unremembered Realms. The beast had been turned to stone by a medusa a few hundred years ago. Its innards were carved out, and the whole creature got converted into a city, called Dragondrop.

The story told is that, in the dragon's old age, it had lost its eyesight and somehow had fallen in love with a medusa. They spent most of their time in Gaspenfall, walking the sands of the Barrendry desert sharing poetry, singing songs, and eating people. Things were going great, until the day of their marriage. The cleric that they hired had to wear a blindfold for the ceremony and grabbed his Cure Blindness staff, by mistake. The ancient dragon got to look upon the beauty of his love only one time. It was for the best, I presume, because the medusa ran off with the cleric and neither were heard from again.

It took gnomes almost a hundred years to carve a city out of the dragon, but when it was complete, it was an amazing place. Shops lined the ribcage and flowered parks ran throughout the center. Fountains poured fresh water and birds sang from perches or nests high above. Thousands of visitors came to this place every year to celebrate the love of the two creatures, tell stories, and do a bit of shopping. The gnomes seemed to be running the entire operation.

As a kid, I had been in here a hundred times and much more as an adult. I remember that my mom would buy me knitted caps from a gnome, named Nissa Nackle Nim. She would sit in her little shop, eating raw potatoes and scratching her silvery-blonde facial hair. She always had a medusa cap ready for my sister and a dragon cap knitted for me.

I hadn't seen the little gnome in years. I heard she took up adventuring, but things change quickly in the realms. As I stood by Nissa's old booth, I happened to look up and see something I had never noticed before. High along the rib cage, in the unlit darkness of the spine, was a bit of rock that was carved like a heart. I asked one of the worker gnomes in a nearby pretzel shop about it and he stared at me for a moment, before stating, "Forget about it. It's nothing. Just leave."

He ran off without another word through the back door of his shop. I asked around at some other shops, but I got the same cold treatment. Then, I began to notice the worker gnomes were now paying attention to my every move, like I was some kind of thief. I sat down in the park and studied the heart for a while. It suddenly occurred to me that I hadn't been in here since I had received my new lich eye. There must be something about this eye that let me notice this dark heart's form.

When I thought the gnomes weren't looking, I slipped behind a food stand and covered myself with my Blending Cloak. From there, I went over to a wall and started climbing up the rib cage toward the heart. My special Spider Climbing ring was handy in times like this. I stopped halfway up and watched the confused gnomes look around the area for me, before I finished crawling up to the heart of stone. I spotted a small dark window and crawled through it.

I kept myself hid quite well, as I padded slowly through this beautifully sculpted chamber. It appeared to be a black marble of some sort. In the center was a green glow that gave a mild illumination to this place. "Do you like my home?" came a voice from the direction of the glowing light. "My love had such a black heart!"

I immediately lowered my head and averted her gaze. It was the medusa! After all these years, she was still alive and in the very heart of the monument she created by mistake. "I'm sorry to hear about your situation," I spoke, while she slithered up to me.

"Don't feel bad, handsome," she replied. "One look at me will remove all your pain."

I stepped back a bit and nearly fell over a small statue. As I looked around, I saw a bunch of these stone figures in various poses. "This is my gnome garden," she explained, while slithering through them. "The gnomes worship me. They sacrifice one of themselves a few times a year to keep me fed."

"It doesn't look to me like you eat them," I observed.

The medusa just laughed. "No, no, rogue. I turn them to stone and drink their life force. It's what keeps me alive!"

With that said, she slithered up and stood before me. I could hear the hisses from the snakes, which made up her hair. "Come now, thief. Hold me. I have no weapons," she claimed, holding open her arms.

I wasn't confident in what I was about to do, but I had to take a risk anyway. I stood up straight, slowly grabbing my dagger, Magurk. I closed my human eye and looked up. She stood there grinning for a moment with her eyes in a greenish glow. Then, she frowned. She noticed my lich eye was also glowing green. Her gaze only worked on the living; my lich eye was a thing of magic; a magical piece of the undead.

Before she could say a word, my blade had found its mark. She crumpled to the floor with a hiss and a soft sigh. I barely got my dagger, Magurk, out of her before she, herself, turned to stone and finally, to a pile of dust. Lying in the dust, was a large black gem in the shape of a heart; which, I did not hesitate to slip into a pouch.

Things seemed different in Dragondrop after that. The gnomes looked more relaxed and at peace. No one, until now, dear reader, ever knew it was me who brought the change. That day, I left the city with a warm pretzel and a cold black heart.

Entry 107

One night, I found myself walking through the streets of Irkruf-fle, a small, forested hamlet to the north of the Hoktu Mountains. It felt like I was in a dream or something, because I did not seem to be in control of myself. One minute, I'd be staring at the stars and chanting some indecipherable gobbledygook and the next, I'd be stealing loose socks from villager's clothes lines.

Most of the time, I stayed hidden, but when I did stroll out into public, people would run in fright or try to attack me outright. The people of the hamlet would shout out all kinds of names, like "pest," "ghost," or "night walker". The weird part is, that they'd throw things at me, and the items would sail straight through my body, like I wasn't even there.

Night after night, I would do horrible things, like tip chamber-pots, take bites of the fruits at the marketplace, clean between my toes with toothbrushes, or even lead a night time cat orchestra to keep the folks up. One night, as I was leading my feline singers in a touching love song, a crowd of villagers gathered around me and were pointing. I stopped leading the cats and turned around to see the villagers leading a cleric and a tough looking dwarf with a large axe toward me.

The cleric stared at me, scratching his head, and lowered his cowl. It was my friend Healy. I tried to say something, but he just couldn't understand, so I flicked him on his ear. "Ow!" he re-sponded. "Gwai Lo!"

I'd heard that nickname before and it jarred me. As I stood there trying to regain my thoughts, the cleric pulled out his mace, threw some sparkle dust over it, and nailed me across the face. The weapon didn't pass through me, this time. I felt it.

This jarring pain woke me from this dreamlike state and I in-stantly sat up. I rubbed my eyes and looked around, realizing I wasn't at that location anymore, but back into my real body. I glanced around and saw green root-like tendrils attached to my legs, chest, and face. I quickly pulled them off of me, only to hear a quite painful moan. As I gathered my wits, I suddenly remembered where I was and why I was there. Before me, stood a tall, dark tree with dark purple leaves and slowly moving branches. It was a Bothersome Tree.

These rare trees were created by lunatic druids who wanted to become one with nature. They were high-level druids that their magic to transfer themselves into these giant wonders of nature and extend their lives by hundreds of years. The problem is, these "disturbovaurs" hijack passersby bodies to "bother" nearby villages and get them to abandon their area, so it can return to nature. I must have fallen asleep under this one a while ago, without realizing it.

"Useful..." the tree spoke slowly. "Powerful."

With that said, more roots came from the ground and wrapped themselves around my legs. "Serve me," it mumbled in a voice that shook inside my head.

"I don't think so," I replied, trying to find my trusty dagger, Magurk. "I should have known what you were by your odor, druid."

The tree laughed, as it wrapped its roots around my arms, pinning them to my side. "Repeat after me," it grumbled, "Yes, my master."

"How about you repeat after me?" I said, as its roots started to embed themselves back in through my skin. "Timber..." I wheezed.

"Timber?" it repeated.

Then, there was a loud thud and the druidic monstrosity flinched. Then, another. The roots fell away from me and the voice that was screaming in my head fell into a fading echo. Standing behind the tree, was Logtoss the Dwarf, whacking at it with his axe. I fell to the ground and rolled away, as the large tree came crashing down.

Healy the Cleric walked up and helped me to my feet. "You okay?" he asked.

"Just a little cold," I said, hoarsely. "Could you start a campfire."

Healy just smiled and waved to the dwarf, who started hacking at some branches. "No bother, at all."

Entry 108

I was dumped into the swamps of Widowsmarsh by a manticore, before it could get me to its lair. It was a good fifty feet or more in the air when it let go of me. I crashed through the branches of some swamp trees, before landing on a patch of soft moss. I was a bit stunned from the impact, but the soreness in my side where the manticore's claw had dug into me was much worse. I didn't realize how deep the talons had gotten, until I slowly removed them. My dagger, Magurk, played a huge part in helping the winged beast decide to release me.

I threw the claw into some nearby swamp water and felt in my cloak for the leftover Healing potion that I had hidden. Making sure I grabbed the right vial, I noticed there were only two swallows left, so I finished off every drop. I could feel the broken rib go back into place and the bleeding stopped, but I was still bruised and incredibly sore. I passed out a few moments later, only to reawaken when I felt my hands and feet were being constricted. When I opened my eyes, I was surrounded by three tall lizard men in white robes. I tried to move, my hands and feet, but they got enveloped with the moss that I had landed on.

"You're lucky we came when we did," hissed one of the lizard men. "This moss would have completely covered you in a couple of hours."

The three creatures looked very pale and sick, some of their scales were peeling off, and they were all missing parts of their tails. "Lepering lizards!" I mumbled, incoherently, as they used their short swords to cut around my hands and feet. I tried scrambling to my feet, but due to the moss and the blood loss, I just managed to pass out again.

When I awoke, I was kneeling with a healthy looking lizard man by a large campfire. The camp became surrounded by dozens of the white-robed lizard men, who were chanting in a lispy drone. Standing before me, was a black-robed dwarf with a rag tied over his face, only revealing his bloodshot eyes. He held a cleric's staff in the air, as he called for a halt to the chanting.

"Welcome to our home, new recruits!" he yelled out. "Where you will soon believe in truth, and all the secrets of the realms will be revealed..."

The white-robed creatures all let out a shout in unison, agreeing with this weird little dwarf. "I see the doubt in your face, rogue," he said, as he walked up to the lizard man and me. "Soon, you will see that I am the cure; I am the one you'll need to continue your journey in this life!"

He pulled my hood back and gave me the once over. He slowly started to smile. "My name is Doomcough. I am the leader of this colony and.."

"Doomcough?!" I interrupted. "That's a dumb name."

The dwarf shook his fist in my face. "Why you...." Then, he took a breath and calmed down.

"Here," he said, walking over to the lizard man. "Watch and learn."

He pulled the rag down from over his mouth and coughed heartily into the lizard man's face. The creature flinched and closed its eyes as phlegm and mucous splattered all over its nose and maw. Within moments, the lizard man started to turn a paler shade of green.

"Get this one a robe," he commanded his lackey's. "He will take his place amongst the others!"

He turned to me, with a grin, and that's when I recognized his face. It was Dimwood the Cleric! I had wondered what happened to him. The last time I saw him was in this very swamp. "I see you now remember who I am," he said, stepping up to me. "And don't think I've forgotten about the little prank you pulled on Argenfall and me."

"That was a good one," I laughed. "Good times."

"I was beaten to a pulp and taken as a slave to the lizard men, you fool!" he yelled at me. "I don't even know what they did with Argenfall!"

I was beginning to suspect that Dimwood was not that fond of me anymore, so I just decided to stall my fate a few moments longer. "How did you end up here?" I asked.

"When they hauled me back to their camp, a shaman nursed me

back to health...sort of," he explained. "When I got well enough, he cast a leprosy spell on me to keep me from running away. I had been acting as a nursemaid for the baby lizards for a while. That is, until I managed to steal a bottle of his homebrewed Cure Disease potion." he said.

"But don't worry, I developed my own cure, in case I ever need it," he added with a wink, as he absent-mindedly tapped an unseen pocket of his robe. "Which turns out, is even better."

He stepped up close and was nearly to my face, as he continued. "I drank the shaman's not-so-effective homebrew, and it did cure me-sort of. Now, whoever I breath on catches leprosy and dies, eventually."

"I don't understand what you're doing here, though," I asked, while slowly peeling the living moss off my human hand. "Why didn't you just run away?"

"Are you kidding?" he hissed at me, inching closer. "This was my one chance for real power! So, I am now Doomcough, leader of my Lepermen Acolytes! "No more Mr. Nice Guy, I'm the one in charge now, Gwai Lo!"

Then, he moved closer and coughed in my face. I quickly put my hand in the dirt and threw some at his eyes. I grabbed the vial from his pocket, jumped up, and then kicked him in the head, knocking him over. As dozens of his acolytes surrounded me, I shoved my other moss covered hand into the fire, which burned the moss away, then held it up for all the lizard men to see. They saw my lizard hand holding a vile.

"It's a miracle!" one exclaimed. "This human is one of us!"

"No!" shouted Dimwood. "Don't listen to him; it's a trick!"

I spun around and popped the cork on the vial. "You want your cure? Come and get it!"

With that, I poured the vial all over Doomwood, or Dimcough, or whatever his name was, and the entire group of lizard men was on him, biting and tearing, trying to get the littlest taste of the cure. I stood back watching for a moment, almost feeling sorry for the little guy.

The lizard men stood up and turned toward me with grins on their faces. "Your fate is sealed, human."

"Wait a minute," I said, stepping back. "I thought I was one with you?"

"We too, know of you, Ghost Man," one said, while looking rather sweaty. "You are diseased; we will help you on your journey into the next life!"

I reached into my pocket and pulled out a vial, "I'll drink to that!" I said, as I quickly gulped the contents of the vial. The lizard men's jaws dropped, as they realized what I had just done. They scrambled over to what was left of Doomcough and picked up the empty vial that I had dropped next to him. "Poison!" they exclaimed.

As they turned and started to lunge for me, they dropped like flies onto the ground. I pulled my hood back over my cloak, walked over to the torn up cleric, and grabbed his magical staff. "This could be worth something," I thought. "Only a dummkopf would leave this behind!"

Entry 109

One of the coolest events in the realms is the Boondoggle Enduro; a massive race that happens once a year and runs a course through all four of the Unremembered Realms. The object of the competition is simply to survive and cross the finish line first. At the end, is a pile of gold and the coveted "Survivor Cup" trophy. I dreamed of racing in one of these events since I was a kid, and I have gotten gold in many ways, so I could participate.

The year I did join the race was a grand one indeed. On day one, I recruited a team of gnomes to build a horseless carriage. These carriages are special ones created by the craftiest Gnoman tinkerers. They are propelled by animal fat and electricity. There is a metal rod, which runs down the center of wagon between all four wheels. This rod, when turned, moves the cogs and gears, like in a clock. When the animal grease is applied, then supercharged with a lightning spell, it drives the wagon forward The speed is determined by the power of the caster.

In cases where your caster runs low on his spells or just gets tired, there is a hand crank in the center with seats on either side. This helps if you need to go manual. The wagon is directed in the front by a wheel, like a steering column of a boat. Sometimes, these wagons, called "land ships," mine even had an emergency sail installed.

I nearly fell over when I got the delivery scroll confirming my acceptance into the race. I worked as fast and furiously as I could to assemble my crew and build my land ship. I had heard rumors about the Fire Gnomes of Darkenbleak being top notch, so I made haste over to the Burnfield Plains. There, I hired the most famous team I could afford, a gnome, named Nitrus Boomshift, and his sidekick, Tork Airhammer. They worked at a wagon shop called "The Pit Stop," which was well known for their top gear engineers.

After the completion of my land ship, which I affectionately named the "Jolt," I made a stop in Eaglespaw to pick up my associates, Healy the Cleric and Fodderman the Zombie. Healy would be able to call lightning from the sky to power the wagon, while Fodderman would be ideal for hand cranking the manual gears when Healy needed breaks. Zombies never get tired, so I thought Fodderman would be the perfect pick for my team.

I secretly purchased a map of shortcuts from Robbie the Thief. I figured it would give me an advantage. Finally, I brought in Bugbeard the Unwashed as navigator. Bugbeard smelled something fierce, but he was a ranger who knew the realms like the back of his stained and crusty hand. Being the captain of the Jolt Ship, I was in charge of steering and keeping the crew working in unison.

The race was to start in the city of Neverspring and end at the Neverspring Bridge. The course map was handed out at the beginning, showing markers where all the participants were to stop. At each station, we had to attain a seal of approval from an official; this guaranteed no one would be skipping routes.

On the big day, over one hundred wagons showed up to participate. I could tell from the armor and weaponry on some of these land ships that there wouldn't be too many of us reaching the finish line.

The race always attracted a wide variety of people who love the thrill of a good race.

There was Baron Tolaren the Dragonborn, in his pitch black

wagon. It was always fun to see a nobleman join in on the fun. Baron was a gruff fellow, but a great competitor.

Along the side of him, was last year's race champion, Movain Moonblade. The wild elf barely crossed the finish line in one piece last year, but it seems his decked out wagon, the War Spirit, had been repaired and pimped out again for this year.

"You turkeys are gonna gobble dust!" shouted a voice from a couple of wagons down. It was Porkenthall the Windbag.

He was at the wheel of a brightly painted eyesore of a wagon labeled with big letters, "The Rune Buggy." I almost laughed at the angry looking butterflies he had crudely hand painted on the sides. I thought that wizard had learned his lesson before, but here he was, louder than ever. "I've brought a couple of your friends!"

Standing up on either side of Porkenthall was Apichat and Onquay, my Crimson Roof Guild brothers. I was wondering how Porkenthall got funding for his wagon. "Elfalfuh sends his regards, Gwai Lo!" Apichat shouted. "I wouldn't count on finishing this race, if I were you!"

Onquay stuck his tongue out at me and I could see the metal stud in the middle of it. I guess Elfalfuh did nail their tongues to the wall. "No hard feelings, then?" I laughed, which seemed to anger them quite well.

After a few other verbal pleasantries, we were all motioned to get ready to roll. With the firing off of the official cannonball, the wagons sprang from their locations and sod flew as the race got underway. A few wagons never made it past the gate, as misengineered gear systems were fried on the spot by the lightning bolts used to propel them. One crew flopped over dead, on account of the engineers had forgotten to ground the system!

Most of our trip through Gaspenfall went smoothly, except when we were sideswiped by a hotshot group of elves who thought they could take us out. We were just on the outskirts of Dragondrop, steering our way through the rocky terrain of the Barrendry Desert. As they came in for a second swipe, I grabbed Fodderman and threw him aboard their land ship. There were lots of screams, as he bit the face of their captain and they steered directly into the side of a massive rock formation.

I swung the Jolt Ship around quickly, snatched up Fodderman, and continued on. I slapped Fodderman on the back, and I thought he gave me a smile. It's hard to tell if a zombie is smiling or not, especially when there's bits of elf hair and brain in his teeth. Things went smoothly for a while after that, well, until we reached Darkmist, that is. There was a checkpoint we had to hit at the dreaded Ruins of Rippenwind. The ruins are a very scary place, so most people of the realms avoid them like the plague.

You never knew what creatures were hanging out in this large metropolis of decay, so it was best just to get in and get out. After getting our scroll marked at the checkpoint, we started heading west toward Eaglespaw. I yelled out for Bugbeard to consult the "Shortcut" map that Robbie sold me and he started guiding us through this dismal area.

I thought we were going to make it through unscathed, but as we cleared the last wall of the ruins, we rode into a dense fog. I closed my left eye and surveyed ahead, using my lich eye. There, in front of us to the left, was a wagon full of orcs aiming bows behind them and straight at us. I pulled hard to the right and most of the arrows sailed right over our heads.

Bugbeard was eating the fleas he picked out of his beard and didn't react in time when I shouted "duck." He immediately fell overboard with an arrow to the face. I watched, in horror, as the shortcut map I needed flew out of his hands and blew off, only to be picked up by the orcs as they circled. "Ha ha ha, human!" a big ugly orc shouted. "Sloptroff say thank you for map!"

The arrogant orc crew sped off in front of us. I knew I could pick up an official map at the next check point, but rumor had it that this area was tricky. Losing Robbie's map was going to hurt. At least, that's what I thought at first, because a few hours later, we passed by Thurston Furblud's vampire castle. And what did we see as the Jolt wagon rolled past? Sloptroff's wagon half sunk into a mud pit, and there was Thurston himself draining the life out of Sloptroff. The ugly orc saw us rolling by and reached out with his hand, so I waved back, "You're welcome!" I yelled, as we circled round the muddy trap. For once, I didn't know whether to strangle Robbie or send him a thank you letter.

There was another checkpoint by Lake Underglub, which we hit way ahead of schedule and the competition was thinning out. Healy told me that Thurston Furblud had probably made a bunch of fake shortcut maps to get his food delivered. He probably gave the maps to Robbie the Thief, who in turn, made good coin duping racing hopefuls like me. I'm just jealous that I didn't think of it first. I suppose Healy was probably right.

Healy napped for a while, as we headed north into Slaphammer, just west of the Hoktu Mountains. The next checkpoint was at Dockport in Winterspring, so I figured Fodderman could hand crank the Jolt ship for a bit, while we rested.

When I woke up, it was to loud crashes and boulders flying everywhere. A massive stone giant had us in his grip and was running us over the mountains as fast as he could run. I looked over at Fodderman the Zombie and he was still mindlessly turning the manual crank. "Healy! Wake up!" I shouted, as the giant barely paid any attention to us. Without hesitation, Healy prepared to blast the giant, while I pulled out my trusty Swatfly bow and notched a poison arrow.

Just then, a large rock flew by the creature's head and he just flinched and kept running. He gave us a quick look and a wink and motioned with his eyes to look behind us. We turned around and saw three other giants in close pursuit; some were carrying boulders to throw at this behemoth carrying us. We also noticed that they were holding racing wagons as well. "You betta win!" muttered the giant, as he huffed and puffed. "Me got big bet on you!"

Healy and I looked at each other, shrugged, and held onto the wagon for dear life. Moments later, the giant leaped over a crevice and was sliding down the side of the mountain, laughing the whole way. When he reached the bottom, he let us go with a wave and grabbed a huge boulder. While the other giants were sliding down, he threw the big rock, and it smashed into a wagon full of screaming Cagin' Dwarves. I never heard what they said, but I guaroontee, I wouldn't have understood it. Cagin' Dwarves had a thick southern accent.

Within two hours, we had checked in at Dockport and made our way east out of the city. We rode safely along the south end of Faerwood Forest. Neverspring was a half-day away, and I had a good feeling that we would be making it to the finish line. I didn't know what place we'd be in. By the time we reached Tanglewood Forest, it was evident that a few wagons were closing in fast. At that rate, they would pass us in only a few hours.

By the time we hit the Neverspring Bridge, Healy was jolting the lightening rod with every ounce of lightening he could conjure. I told Fodderman to jump to the manual crank, while I defended our rear from the Rune Buggy, which was now breathing down our necks. The finish line was just ahead, so the pressure was mounting!

Apichat shouted slurs at us, while steering, as Porkenthall shot lightning bolt after lightning bolt to increase their power. Onquay didn't seem to notice us; he was slumped over in his seat, looking pale. He had a half open shortcut map in his hand and a vampire bite mark on his neck.

As we sped side-by-side over the bridge into Neverspring, Apichat gave me a grin, as he pulled a bottle with a flaming rag in it and threw it at our wagon.

Being quite nimble, I jumped over and slammed it out of the air and onto the bridge below the two carts. It was all a blur, what happened next, because there was a loud explosion. Both of our land ships blew into the air in a cloud of smoke and fire. Luckily, I hit the water below the bridge. When I gathered my wits and crawled my way onto the bank, I heard the trumpets sounding that the race had ended. I was not happy.

Through the thunderous applause, I heard Healy calling out for me, so I met him by the flaming steering wheel of our wagon. "We lost!" I declared, through my coughs. "Porkenthall has pulled it off!"

Healy shook his head and pointed to the burning wreckage of the Rune Buggy. Porkenthall was trying to put out his burning robes, and Apichat stood yelling at a blank-faced Onquay, who just sat on the ground drooling. "If we didn't win," I asked Healy, "Who did?"

We made a run to the gate of the city to see what had happened.

Along the way, we noticed two burning trail tracks on the ground. Healy let out a whoop and I smiled, as we saw Fodderman standing in the midst of a cheering crowd. He was half covered with flowers and surrounded by fans as we reached him. His expression was the same as it always was, so I pushed his lips up into a smile. Healy tapped my shoulder and pointed to what was left of the Jolt ship. Two wheels and the manual crank column. It was still smoking.

We ended up giving the Survivor Cup to our zombie friend and hung around the city for a while. I didn't hear what happened to Apichat, Onquay, or Porkenthall after that; I figured they were sitting in some local tavern sharing a big bowl of sour grapes.

Entry 110

It started out like any other day – conflict, confusion, chaos, time in jail. I had been behind bars in Port Laudervale many times, so the constable knew me pretty well. I could escape anytime I wanted from this little dive, but I used it as a chance to catch up on some sleep. I never got too mad about my punishments, he had a job to do and so did I, such was the nature of the game.

I even got to know his family and looked forward to hearing about their lives; which, were much different than mine. On cold, rainy nights Constable Bogetow's wife, Cornelia, would even sneak me in an extra blanket, a warm meal, and to my joy, some nibble delights. "How's the family?" I'd ask.

"Things aren't too good in Port Laudervale right now," she stated. "Hubby's been doing a lot of overtime, since the new mayor has taken over. We hardly see him anymore."

"A mayor? What happened to Mayor Udderglove?" I inquired. "Everybody liked him."

"That's what's strange," Cornelia explained. "His term was up, so he began his usual campaign. But then, a challenger came into town by the name of Roy Drayge. Claimed to be some hotshot from Neverspring. Yet, none of the folks around here ever heard of him."

"Me neither," I replied.

"Well, one night during the debates in the town square, Mayor Udderglove started saying these awful things, really awful!" she claimed. "He started confessing to crimes he'd never committed and even started insulting our mothers."

"That doesn't sound like him," I commented.

Cornelia nodded in agreement. "What was so bizarre about the whole thing, was that his tirade almost sounded like singing, and he had this horrible look on his face, like he couldn't stop himself from speaking."

"What was Roy Drayge doing all that time?" I asked.

"He was just going over his notes and mumbling quietly to himself," she answered. "And ever since he's won the election, he's been on a rampage, overworking us, overtaxing us, you name it."

Cornelia picked up my empty plate and opened the cell door. "I wish someone who was sneaky enough could find out more about Mayor Drayge. This town could use the help. My poor Balga's being worked half to death."

"Isn't there a new election coming up?" I asked. "Just have your husband run against him; he's bound to win."

"He's scared," she explained. "Rumor has it, that Mayor Drayge is using some kind of magic. What if he destroys my husband, socially, along with his good reputation?"

When she closed the cell door, she left it open just an inch. When I snuck out through the front, I noticed all my gear set neatly on a table and the jailor and his wife casually talking to each other, with their backs to me, as they looked out a window. I just smiled and headed out the door in the direction of the mayor's mansion.

From what I knew of Mayor Roy Drayge , he was a laid back guy, until you made him angry or disagreed with him in any way. I knew his manor was heavily guarded and I didn't want to take him head on. He held a high position and I had already had bad run-ins with other mayors, so I knew I needed help. Within in a couple of days, I arrived in Neverspring, right at the front door of the Palm Eye Finger Magic Shop.

The shop was rebuilt almost two years after the fire that was set

169

by the unruly druids when I was a kid. I'd been back a few times here and there, and Bub and Lar were still there, older yes, but still full of pranks. Bub stroked his long white beard and listened intently, while I explained the situation. Lar listened, nodded, and ran from book to book looking for something. When I finished my story, Lar nodded his bald head and held up a finger.

"I know how he's doing it," explained the magical inventor, as he hauled over a large dusty tome; which, he plopped down on a table. He thumbed through a bunch of pages and stopped at one written in a language that I couldn't recognize.

"Remember this?" Lar asked Bub.

Bub squinted at the page closely and smiled. "My, my, my," he muttered. "It's your Wordbending scroll!"

They both started giggling and shuffling about the room, singing and waving their arms around like conductors. I waited for their little show to end and asked, "What are you two talking about?"

"It was one of my best pranks," exclaimed Lar. "We had so much fun with it!"

"I thought it was lost with the shop on the night of the druid fire," stated Bub. "I'm so excited to hear that it has survived!"

I sat there, frowning, while they finally explained. "The scroll has a variety of letters and notes," Lar stated, as he pointed to symbols on the page. "You manipulate them by pressing the letters and muttering their sounds!"

Bub added. "This scroll has the uncanny ability to automatically tune a target's voice until you are in complete control of what they are saying. The fun part is, it comes out of their mouth all sing-songy."

"That explains how Udderglove was manipulated to say the things that he did," I said, as I started pacing the room. After a few moments, I stopped, and a large grin grew on my face.

"If you have a plan," Bub stated. "We're in."

After explaining the situation in full detail, Bub and Lar were thrilled that they could be a help. Lar dug out a spell book, while Bub sifted through a large pile of scrolls. Lar read from his book and a shimmering black door opened next to him. When I peered through the door, I could see a little room with stockpiles of gold all around. In the center of the room, was an intricately carved small wooden table with a scroll laid on top of it.

"I can't hold this doorway long," he said, breaking out in a sweat. "You need to hurry."

"Here," Bub said, handing me a scroll. "Replace it with this!"

I grabbed the scroll and headed through the doorway. I was instantly transported into the treasure room of Mayor Roy Drayge. I grabbed the Wordbending scroll and replaced it with the one Bub had given me. I had no idea what it said and I didn't care to find out. Out of the corner of my eye, I spotted a large diamond with an emerald somehow embedded in its core. It fit in my pocket, perfectly. Within moments, I stepped back through the doorway and into the room with the two crazy magicians.

Bub and Lar fawned over the scroll for a bit, before I left to complete the second half of my plan.

The next month brought a fierce campaign between Mayor Drayge and Head Constable Balga Bogetow. The Mayor had been pulling every dirty trick in the book, but I knew what his plans were for the big debate. I assured Constable Bogetow and his wife that things would go well that night, and did they ever!

Mayor Drayge took the stage and cheers from his paid off sycophants roared out with applause. He carried a scroll with him to the stage and stood behind the polished oak podium to the crowd's left. The constable, on the other hand, hid in the back with a small group of his force. I quietly donned my Hat of Disguising and made myself appear to be Constable Bogetow. Cornelia even walked with me to the podium, waving to the onlookers. I, too, carried a scroll.

After brief introductions, the moderator allowed Mayor Drayge to make his opening statement, which gave me a chance to test my scroll. "To the kind citizens of Port Laudervale," he began, "I just want to let you know that I love to sniff my horrid socks."

Laughter from the crowd ensued at this statement, the mayor turned red in the face, and looked at me in shock. I smiled back and gave a little hand wave. "I use all the taxes for underarm waxes," he began to sing, "And let's not forget this crowd's mothers, who reek worse than a hog's brother, and their smell could sail ships, if they could handle the whiff. But, what my constituents lack in brains, they make up for with tooth stains, and a horde of undead looks better than all you inbreds, but hey, line up and donate your gold...la la la."

Roy Drayge was beet red and now facing a furious mob. Even his paid sycophants started booing. The moderator managed to calm the crowd down and said "Now, let's hear from the mayor's opponent, Head Constable Bogetow. As I started speaking, Drayge quickly opened his scroll and started muttering as fast as he could. Within moments, a twinkling blue light formed around the mayor and he transformed into a large angry looking hog. "So, he finally revealed his true identity," I said, as the crowd cheered.

Bub's "Polymorph Yourself Into a Pig" spell scroll was a success! I'm sure he'd be pleased as punch about this. "Long live Mayor Bogetow" shouted the crowd, as they rushed the stage.

I feigned back and stepped behind the curtain for a moment to let the real Balga Bogetow step forward and wave to all his new constituents. I slipped off the hat and into the night. I wish I could have stayed, though. I heard they had an excellent pig roast as part of the celebration.

Entry 111

Never underestimate the opportunities that come from being tortured. The rack is a confessional to most evil doers, and they can't resist running at the mouth, like they've been waiting to talk for years. The torturer will tell you all their plans, what they've already done, where their treasure is, you name it.

They do this, because they believe you aren't going to make it out alive, so it gives someone like me a great chance to cash in on their arrogance. For example, there was an evil wizard by the name of Hackinweez, who was gathering up resources in Winterspring. His goblin army was growing into the thousands and it was scaring the people of Farlong. The king of Farlong spent most of his free time dreamwelding on the Isle of Fortune, so his main army was pretty much at a standstill.

Rumor had it, that Hackinweez was building a nice sized stone fortress near the town of Bellowmoan. I was getting low on funds, so I decided to pay the wizard a visit.

First, I tried things the hard way, using my Blending Cloak to sneak past the guards at night and locate the hidden treasure room. I didn't have much luck with that, so I decided to try the torture method, instead. I was listening carefully for some moans and eventually, found the torture chamber. It wasn't hard, though; it was at the lowest level, as usual.

I snuck in the torture room, hid my equipment, then tiptoed out and found a guard to punch in the face. Within moments, I was being piled on by other guards, and I was hauled onto a torture rack to wait for the big boss. Sure, I got beat up a little, that's the name of the game, but when you're as skilled an entrepreneur as I, you can be very creative.

Within an hour, old Hackinweez showed up, leaning on his staff. He was your typical wizard – old, white beard, and long and bony fingers. The torture master pulled the table up, so I was face-to-face with the old coot. Hackinweez started yelling at me, so to appease the fool, I pretended to care and even acted as though I was worried. I knew he was powerful, but that doesn't mean anything to me. You see, the problem with wizards is that they build their confidence around the power of their magic, instead of the wit of their brain.

"What happens now?" I asked, shakily, knowing this was irresistible to the egotistical maniac.

"I'm going to take over the realms!" Hackinweez cackled.

Over the next hour, he laid out his entire plan – where he was going to attack first, who his inside soldiers were in the different towns, and where his fortresses of secret treasures were. I kid you not, by the end, I knew even his grocery list; which, for some reason, had a lot of onions. The torture master, an ugly goblin with a scab the size of a pie on his face, stood next to the stretching rack that I was lying on with his hand on the lever.

"Make sure he suffers slowly," he told the goblin. "I want the others to know who runs the show around here."

"Any last words, fool?" he said, dragging his long fingernails down my face, leaving four trails of blood.

"Thank you," I muttered through gritted teeth.

The goblin looked at me with a big smile. I smiled back, unnerving the foul creature. "I'll keep my eye on this one, Boss," the goblin stated, in a broken version of common.

"Good," the wizard replied. "I'm taking the bulk of our troops to raid a local village for more funds."

"I hope you're not dead by the time I return, I wouldn't mind killing you, myself," Hackinweez declared, before turning and walking out the door.

Neither the wizard nor the scabby goblin had noticed when I used my minor telekinesis power (that I attained while at Big Al's Alchemy Shop) to lift the keys off the goblin. When pie face went and closed the door behind his master, he turned around with a grin, only to see the last thing in this world he would ever see...the razor sharp tip of Magurk pointing at his eye. He had said he'd keep an eye on me, which he did, well, until I wiped it off on my pant leg.

After that, I released the other torture victims in the room and we waited a bit for the old wizard to leave the fortress with his troops. Escaping was easy, most goblins are half deaf and easy to backstab. The prisoners helped me carry treasure, battle maps, and whatnot to the stables where we loaded up everything into goblin war wagons. We headed off to the city of Bellowmoan, where we, after hiding our share of gold, let the authorities know about Hackenweez and his strategies.

By the time the old wizard returned with the goods from his local raid, he had found himself facing the king's army at his own fortress. Half of the goblins ran away, while the others surrendered as the guardians of Winterspring surrounded them. Hackenweez was taken to the gallows, and a noose placed around his neck. The hangman was waiting for his order, when I climbed the stairs. "Any last words?" I asked.

"Why, yes." he began. "I would have taken over the realm if it wasn't for you meddling..."

That's when I signaled the hangman and he pulled the lever.

Entry 112

I had recently been relaxing at the Dice Tower Tavern and playing some games with a human fighter, named Vasel, and an Elven rogue, named Summerer. We had played for a month or so, before they were hired to go raid a dungeon. After a couple of days, I was kind of bumming and needed a gaming fix, but then, I spotted a flyer pinned up on a village community board. It read "Total Strategy Roleplaying presents game night at Grenadier Keep." That was enough for me; I was getting stir crazy and playing games provided some escape from the real world.

I grabbed a little tag off the flyer and thumbed a ride on some caravan; which, dropped me off within a half mile of the place. As it happens, a couple of others on the caravan were on their way there, as well. There was a pimple faced elf, named Clarazel, and an overweight human, named Notzobuff. Notzobuff had kind of an odor, so I made sure I stayed upwind.

The high, gray walls of the keep seemed foreboding, but I'm sure you can guess by now, that I didn't let that stop me! I knocked on the large double doors and waited for someone to answer. We were met at the door by a guy, named Gax. "Welcome to the Grenadiers Keep," he said, cheerfully. Gax was your average looking human, who seemed pleasant enough. He took special care to ask us our names and what were our occupations; which, he quickly wrote down. He guided us through the keep, while telling me every detail about it. He went on about how wide the hallways were, what sat in each corner of the room, the size of the windows, and if the rooms were lit with torches (which, I thought was strange, because I could see that for myself).

Finally, he led us in marching order down into the basement, or lower level, of the keep. We entered a large room with a nicely carved wooden table. Sitting in a chair waiting for us, was a large, angry looking human wearing a spiked war helmet. Next to him, rested an oversized bladed sword, stained with blood. "This is the son of Arn; he's one of our game's developers." Gax explained.

Next, he pointed to a gnome wearing really thick glasses, who was sculpting something small. He barely looked up when Gax introduced him by name. "This is Raul Partha; he's sculpting miniature figures for this games system."

The whole scene at this place seemed innocent enough. "The game is called Automatic Death & Dismemberment," Gax explained, as we sat down. "Basically, it's a roleplaying system that may or may not kill you by the end of the game. It really hasn't caught on yet, but we're hoping that, through this playtesting group, we can work out the bugs."

I didn't know it yet, but this game was going to be more brutal than "Rogue Roullette;" which, is popular among my Crimson Roof Guild brothers. Gax showed everyone how to "roll up" characters using dice. I assured Gax that I was no stranger to role playing games, so I didn't need any babysitting.

When the game finally started, our characters made their first random encounter in the woods against some made up fantasy creatures. Notzobuff's character jumped up to face the challenge, but the player himself made a couple of bad rolls. His character died quickly, with what Gax called a "fumble." At this moment, Arn's son got up from the table with his large sword and dismembered the sweaty human in just a few strokes.

I took a few notes and the game continued. It wasn't long before Clarazel rolled bad and shouted "My dice are out to kill me," as Arn's son slashed the oily elf to pieces.

Raul never looked up from his sculpting and Gax acted like this was the most natural thing in the world. That's when I realized what the problem was. "Have you ever considered changing the rules of this, (using air quotes) Automatic Death & Dismemberment system? Maybe, to where the player doesn't get hacked to pieces, if their character dies?"

Gax, Arn's son, and Raul just stared at me for a minute; not even blinking. They rushed into a corner and formed a huddle. They came back to the table a moment later and Gax spoke, "We never even considered that for Automatic Death & Dismemberment!" he said, in a surprised tone. "Do you have any other ideas?"

The three of them sat taking notes, while I told them of some of my thoughts. I even lifted a few dungeon crawl stories from this very journal to give them inspiration. They seemed pretty giddy about the whole idea. Raul Partha liked the stories with dragons so much, that he started carving a miniature one right there on the spot. I even recounted a tale of this creep on the Borderlands that I met. "I like where this is going," Gax interrupted my tale. "It's much more advanced than the old system. Perhaps I should rename it."

Even Arn's son shook my hand. "Thank you for your help, Rogue," he stated. "I'm sure this game will be an overnight sensation!"

The game really didn't gain much traction, at first, just some creative folk with big imaginations playing in their basements. Eventually, it gained more popularity though, and I'd even see it in a store or two when I was out "picking things up." People who know the secret history of the game will ask me, from time to time, if it bothers me that they've written a parody of some of my stories. I don't mind really, imitation and parody are the sincerest forms of flattery, in my book.

Entry 113

I had just left another failed attempt to raid the Temple of Temperamental Evil and was headed west toward one of the many "stow-n-go's" that I have hidden throughout the realms. Most of these are just chests that I've buried in the ground at secretly mapped out locations. I'll keep gold, extra clothing, potions, poisons, antidotes, and other useful things. You never know for sure what the future holds, so it's always best to be prepared.

It was still nightfall, when I crossed the border into Moonwink and made my way through the thick forest to my secret "stow-n-go" location. It wasn't easy digging up my supplies, considering I had a broken arm, some cracked ribs, and my face was all black and blue. The last battle at the temple was a doozie. My party and I encountered a large cyclops, who killed off a few of us, before the rest could escape.

When I finally managed to get the chest open, I painfully sighed in relief. Three healing potions. I drank one down, immediately, and waited for the effects. My arm reset itself and soon I was able to breathe again. I wasn't completely healed yet; the soreness had made me consider drinking a second one. As my breathing steadied, I could still hear loud breathing that I didn't realize wasn't coming from me. I held my breath a moment to try to stop the sound, but it kept going. That's when I jumped back and pulled out Magurk.

Just off to my left, about ten feet away, was a man stumbling towards me slowly, breathing quite heavily. He looked like a human ranger, or what was barely left of one. His face looked badly scarred and he was mumbling incoherently. "Lobo....sphere... curse..."

Within a few feet of me, he crumpled to the ground and looked like he was about to die. I reluctantly grabbed one of my valuable healing potions, uncorked it, and poured it down his throat. Potions are expensive these days and this chump might not be someone the world needs around anyway, but I like taking risks. Within a few moments, the ranger came to and blinked at me with the one eye that wasn't swollen shut.

"Lobotomus," he said, slowly. "The cursed sphere."

"What are you talking about?" I asked, as I helped him to lean his back onto a tree.

"I just came from a quest to find the Infinity Sphere," he sputtered, after a mild coughing fit. "I know it's location."

Infinity Sphere? I hadn't heard of that before. It sounded powerful, though- powerfully valuable! "It's cursed," he continued. "It always destroys its possessor. I was part of a team sent to demolish it."

"Whatever happened, it must have been bad," I stated. "Because, you are in pretty rough shape."

"Lobotomus, the Mind Slayer, caught wind of our quest and used his abilities to track my team down," he explained. "He wants the Infinity Sphere for himself, so he can use it to destroy and then enslave the world."

Mind Slayers. They are rare, but horrid creatures who go around the realms using their tentacle-like mouths to wrap around the skulls of their victims and suck out the minds. They gain the knowledge of the victim and then, leave them in a comatose state to just die on their own.

"It looks like he tried to eat your mind, judging the condition of your face," I said. "How did you get away?"

"He almost ate the part of my mind with the exact location of the sphere," he explained. "But, this barbarian came running out of the woods and punched him in the face, knocking him backward."

"His name is YaMacha," I grinned. I had figured he'd be one who survived the cyclops.

"Lobotomus and his followers started chasing him, and that's how I got away. I hope he managed to escape, too," the ranger stated. "I don't know who you are, stranger, but we have to destroy the sphere, before Lobotomus finds it."

"He doesn't know where it is?" I asked.

"He's probably closing in on its location," he continued. "But if we can beat him there, we can get the sphere before he does."

Before I could ask, he adjusted his cloak, and with a few groans, stood up. "It's in a cave, just beyond this grove of trees," he said. "By the way, stranger. My name Crumb Duff, I'm a ranger out of Rippenwind. What's your name?"

"That doesn't matter, right now," I explained. "Let's get this Infinity Sphere and get out of Moonwink."

I helped him walk the short distance to the cave entrance. A dozen or so corpses were lying on the ground in front of it. Some were sliced clean open, while others had mind slayer scars over their faces. "He must have been here already and taken the treasure!" I exclaimed.

Crumb Duff hobbled up to the entrance and pointed to some runes carved into the entryway's frame. "These are magic runes that the elves put up to keep mind slayers out. They knew such an item would be ultra-powerful for the frightening creatures, so they put up a barrier that doesn't let them pass."

"That was smart," I remarked. "Now let's get in there and get that sphere."

With that, Crumb started coughing and fell to a knee. I ran over to help, as he sat on the ground. "Please," he said. "Go on without me. I trust you."

I handed him a vial from my pack and said "Don't drink this unless you absolutely need it. I'll be back in a second."

He started coughing again and waved me on, so I turned around and walked into the cave entrance. At first, it seemed like a small cave, with nothing significant about it. Then, I spotted small holes in the walls. Poison darts. Easy enough. I used my Ring of Spider Climbing to crawl up the ceiling to avoid stepping on any triggers.

Once on the other side, I pushed an odd looking stone and a doorway opened up into a long, smelly, circular corridor. I closed my living eye, so my lich eye could scan the darkness ahead and noticed, about fifteen feet in front of me, were a couple of fresh bodies that were cut completely in half. I lowered myself to the floor, and about halfway down, these large circular blades whooshed over the top of my head.

When I finally made it to the other side, I spotted the Infinity Sphere on a pedestal in the middle of the room. As I cautiously approached it, I could see that it was a round, pitch black sphere. I was surprised by the little white circle painted on it, with the infinity symbol in black on that. When I stood above it, I noticed there was a clear, circular window that was cut into the side, showing some inky, magic water that filled the sphere. Upon closer inspection, I could see a white object with words on it, floating about on the inside.

I picked it up and moved it around in my hands, watching the object move around slowly inside of it. I looked around to make sure nothing was going to jump out of the shadows; then, I shook the Infinity Sphere. "Will I survive this?" I asked the little black ball.

"It is decidedly so" read the words on the small object inside the sphere.

"Are you sure?" I asked, feeling under confident, but amused, as I shook it again.

"Signs point to yes" was the answer that popped up next.

That's when I heard the rumble and noticed the giant round boulder move forward and start its decent toward my location. It's a good thing I had my enhanced Boots of Speed on, because I ran down the corridor with the Infinity Sphere in my hand and barely avoided the blades. With the rolling boulder only seconds behind, I practically flew across the darted floor. I could hear the ricochet of the darts, as they bounced off the boulder.

With one giant leap, I jumped through the small entrance door and I hit the ground face down in the grass. The crash of the boulder, being stuck in the entrance, made a loud boom that created an echo through the trees. Within seconds, I felt the Infinity Sphere lift from my hands. As I looked up, I saw Crumb Duff staring at me, with a giant grin. Before my eyes, I watched as he dropped whatever magic illusion he had and revealed himself as the Mind Slayer, Lobotomus.

His greasy face tentacles shook with laughter, as he shook the ball and showed me what it read "Outlook not so good." I was almost worried, but I saw the empty vial lying on the ground in front of me. "I think it just predicted your fate, not mine," I told him, as I slowly stood up.

"A little bit of your weak poison can't kill me," it gasped, as it shot a magic bolt into my chest, knocking me backward. "How did you know I wasn't human?"

I could feel the burning in my chest, as I sat back up, "One, you wouldn't go into the forbidden cave, and two, I have the eye of a lich, your illusion flickered on and off!"

"I was going to save a little bit of your mind, fool," Lobotomus said, as he strode forward. "But I'm feeling a little weaker, because of that poison. Come, rogue, let me consume all of your thoughts!"

As I scuttled backward, I saw two arrows impale themselves into the chest of this nightmarish figure. "Don't mind the thief!" Bok and Choy, the Ninja Archers, said in unison. "It's YaMacha you might want to pay attention to!"

Lobotomus screamed out in pain and broke both arrows off in anger, as he stopped and saw whatever it was behind me. Running at full steam, was YaMacha Derschingler, in full rage mode. The mind slayers tentacles drooped a bit and he muttered something, as the barbarian landed the first punch. "I'm glad he's on our side," said Choy, as we watched blow after blow crush the head of the creepy beast.

"Wait!" I shouted! "Don't crush the Infinity Sphere!"

I got up and hobbled over, only to see the pile of mess that used to be Lobotomus and the shattered pieces of what could have been the most powerful magic item I'd ever seen. YaMacha stood up, with a big grin on his face. In his right hand, he held the floatable piece that had all the word inscriptions. Before I could ask if there was anything salvageable about the item, I could read the words on the piece he held. "My sources say no."

Entry 114

Wizards are, by far, among the strangest group of people in all the realms. While I do respect many of them, they do turn evil, once in a while, and have to be dealt with. Maybe, it's because they tend to be more book smart than street smart.

Most of them are cheapskates, too. I think it's due to the fact that spell components are expensive and hard to come by. I've watched many mages cut corners to do their craft. I can't even count how many times I've seen some powerful spellcaster brown bagging his lunch on some dungeon crawl. Most won't admit it, but you'd be shocked to know how many still live in their parents' cellar.

A lot of these stresses lead to high blood pressure, so clerics tend to recommend time off to their magic using patients. Vacations aren't usually cheap in the realms, so most of the spellcasters are looking for a way to affordably relax and have fun. Don't get me wrong, there are plenty of successful wizards out there, but most are the put your robe on one arm at a time sort of blokes, who are just trying to make ends meet.

That's where I come in. For a while, I ran a time share scam that I'd use on evil wizards who were rising in power. I would catch wind of them plaguing local cities and I'd travel there, as fast as I could. I knew that the wizards were probably strapped for cash, but eager to have their vacations as well. Knowing what they were up to, I'd head to the local spell component shop in their area. I'd ask if I could leave "Win a Contest" boxes at their store for a small price. I could almost guarantee that I'd have more than a few dozen names dropped in the box every month.

I'd show the store owner my list and he'd point out who the biggest scumbags were. I would pay each one a visit, explaining how they could affordably have a beautiful vacation house on the south side of Moonwink; which, was located on the ocean shore-line. I'd invested some money into said house and had owned it for years, but they didn't know that. All they cared about was the beach, the view, and relaxing in the in ground pool.

Most evil wizards bought into this and I was able to live on a few of their gold coins for a while, without stabbing anybody. I would give them a scheduled date on when they could use the house and these fishies were quite happy with the lines I fed them! I could see in their eyes that they had ulterior motives; i.e., steal the house and kill me. Those thoughts didn't bother me, though. Mostly, be-cause I kept a water blue, man-eating gelatinous cube in the swim-ming pool. Once a month, I'd travel to Moonwick to pick a pair of lightning bolt patterned swim trunks out of the pool and rum-mage through the gear of whatever the rube brought with him.

Entry 115

Not every part of Barrendry is desert. To the northeast, is a sec-tion that is a little bit of paradise. Beautiful trees, beaches, and a healthy climate. Because Barrendry is mostly gnomes, you're bound to run into a disturbed one, sooner or later, especially if they are disturbed by you breaking into their house.

I had traveled to the area, because Robbie the Thief had a hot tip on a crazy gnome, named Goldberg, who lived in a secluded man-sion on the outskirts of Watercliff. Word from the locals was that this little guy was even scaring off the dangerous centicorns, who roam the woods around his place. Some folks claimed he was ei-ther incurably mad or a super genius. I didn't care which; I just heard he had an obsession with gold.

Finding his place was tricky, but once I got there, breaking in was easy. Probably, because the front door opened as soon as I stepped up to it. I felt one of the stones in the walkway beneath my feet

183

shift back into place, as soon as I stepped off of it. When I walked through the entryway, the door closed quietly behind me. I was a bit awestruck by the lack of furniture in the foyer. There were these sketch prints that were pinned to the walls, as well; hundreds, as a matter of fact.

"This nut is really into devices," I mumbled to myself, as I examined a drawing. That's when a tile under my feet lit up and opened. I found myself sliding down a tunnel, then out onto the floor of a tiny room. Before I could stand up, I heard a loud click. The room started to fill with green gas and everything went black.

I don't know how much time had passed, but when I woke up, I was shackled to a wall in a large room filled with the craziest device I had ever seen. "What do you think?" asked the gnome who approached me.

"Allow me to introduce myself," he started. "My name is Goldberg and I'm being funded by the most diabolical wizards, clerics, and military to build the greatest traps in all of the Unremembered Realms."

"Obviously," I replied, looking with amazement at the elaborate contraption that stood before me. Bits of steam were floating above it and I could hear whizzing sounds coming from its middle.

"It's as powerful as it is entertaining," he said, as he walked around me. "This isn't so much a trap, as it is a fun way to die."

"What's with the metal claw pointing at my chest," I asked.

"It's a de-skinner," he said, tapping the metal claws razor sharp blades. "After the blades slice up your skin, the claws tear it off you in one pinch!"

I rudely interrupted his giggling, "Those claws look cheap to me," I started, "You must have used cheap drig parts."

The little gnome turned dark red, climbed a stool, and got into my face. "I never use cheap material. I am an artist, a gift to the...."

"Do you eat orc droppings," I taunted. "Your breath smells like it."

The gnome spun around, not noticing that I now had the shackle keys and one of his gold coins in my hand. He had gotten close enough for me to use my little telekinesis ability. Goldberg then ran over to a small red button and gave it a light tap. With a loud hum, a twang sounded, and a little ball bearing rolled from its resting place. It looped around a track, until it hit a lever that shot a dart into the air. The dart popped a balloon; which, released a gas that floated up toward a candle that instantly ignited with a "foompf," which lit a wick.

Goldberg was so enamored with his creation that he did not see me unlock my shackles. I kept standing there, pretending to be his prisoner, as he followed the mechanical tricks of his device. I swear, he started to drool, as a cup on a chain lifted a small seed down a little waterway, until it hit a stop that blocked the water flow. As the water level rose, it drained over another side; which, hit a sponge that tilted a scale; which, opened a cage door and released a small bird. The bird flew down and grabbed the seed, which was glued to a flotation device. As the bird lifted the entire thing, it uncorked the bottom of the miniature pool and started to drain out the water. "It's on a chain!" cheered the happy gnome, pumping his fist in the air.

"I tried a worm, but it kept wiggling into the water..." he explained to me, like I cared.

After about twenty minutes, the contraptions had mostly been set off and all that was left was a couple of gears and a small cannonball; which, was poised to fall on the "On" switch of the death claw. Goldberg was hopping up and down, by this point, and was nearly crying tears of joy into his cap, when all of a sudden, the cannonball froze in place. "What???!!!" he cried out.

"Cheap drig parts," I said, smugly. "Shouldn't have cut corners, eh?"

"Be quiet!" he yelled, while grabbing a step ladder to examine why it got stuck. He climbed the ladder and began to look over the gear. "Don't worry, my love; I'll fix you."

While his back was turned, I snuck up from behind and put a sleeping hold on the kooky gnome. He struggled for a bit, then went limp. When he woke, a few minutes later, he found himself shackled to the wall. "Wh..what happened?" he asked.

"All the excitement wore you out," I stated. "But, the good news is, I fixed and reset your contraption for you."

"You did?" he smiled. "Thank you! I was worried she was ill!"

"Naw, she's fine," I explained. "She just had a gold coin stuck in her gear...the one just below this cannonball. So, I fixed it."

The gnome suddenly snapped out of his lunacy and could see his predicament. "I don't know who you are, but I've got gold; plenty of it. It's all yours. Let's make a deal."

"What do you think I am?" I replied. "Some kind of rube, Goldberg?"

"I could make you rich!" he screamed at my back, as I walked away.

I paused for a moment, just before I walked out of the room. Without turning around, I flipped the coin into the air behind me. "Heads or tails and I'll let you go."

"Heads! Heads!" he yelled, as the coin hit the little red button.

As the machine started to hum, I walked out the door and shut it. I don't know which side it landed on; I honestly didn't care. I had some gold to find.

Entry 116

I had finally discovered where my mother was hiding – Elflanta Sea Island. It was rumored to be one of the best resort islands in all of the four realms. It was run by some powerful magic using rhakasa (a half-tiger/half man), named Mr. Roark, and his little were rodent sidekick, named Ratu. The upper crust make the journey across the Elflantic Sea to this getaway and are usually never seen again.

There's nothing nefarious about the place; it's just that it's a rich, peaceful environment, from which no one returns. The only way to get there is by supply boat, and these are heavily guarded. Since I had no interest in seeing the crazy old bird, I would stop by the docks and write her letters; which, was a common way to communicate with family or friends living there.

By the time I would return to the area, Mother would usually have a reply waiting for me at my designated "inbox," and this became our routine of irritating one another. The only problem was, when the fishing trolls started to appear and began cutting into our messages. The sailors claimed that their boats would be over-run by these creatures when they got halfway to the island, but I'm not so sure I believe them.

For example, I had written Mother with a very friendly threat and by the time she wrote back cursing the day I was born, there was a comment by some clown, named Basement Banthuh. His add-on to the letter stated that he was making fifteen coins extra per week by staying at home, sorting a clerical temple's billing.

These fishing trolls got so bad, that the port authority decided to step in and start monitoring the letters. This idea was absurd to me, so I quit writing Mother, altogether. I'm sure she was mad that I stopped writing to her, but I was sick of all the politics of this communication, so I closed my Sea Mail account and left.

Entry 117

What is the deal with paladins? Each one seems lost in their world of rules, tactics, and justice. I happen to have my way of op-erating and I cringe whenever someone invites a paladin to our raiding party. For example, there was a growing orc threat rising out of Nabiscove, the hip, new village in Moonwink. As their forces were building, I paid a visit to see what was cooking.

I met with a fresh party at the Tollhouse Tavern, and we all agreed to raid one of the orcs scouting posts that had just popped up. We agreed that, first thing in the morning, we would go out, do a bit of hack and slash, and come back to the tavern to divide the spoils. Voordman was the fighter, a tough looking guy with a colorful shield. Keeblur was a well-known elven mage, who lived in a large tree with others of his kind. Finally, there was a female ranger, named Miss Fields, who was as deadly as she was sweet. The plan seemed to crumble when Voordman had to ruin every-thing by inviting his cousin Hydrocks, the Paladin. I could tell, right away, that he was a bad cookie.

I don't mind paladins, if they know their place, but this guy was hot out of the temple and never given a chance to cool down. He started on about what we should do, giving us ingredients of a plan for what he felt was the best way to take the enemy, but to me, it was just a recipe for doom.

That night, we stayed at the tavern to get some rest, before the inevitable raid. Being a night owl, I went out for a stroll and to pick out a few things from what I call my "walking market." I got to bed around 3:00 a.m. and was barely into a dream, when I heard pounding on the door. "Get up, troops," I heard Hydrocks shout. "It's 3:30 a.m. Time to get up!"

I stumbled, bleary-eyed, out into the hall where I met the rest of the sleep-deprived party. They were rubbing their eyes and yawning when I started for the doorway that led to the dining hall. "Where are you going, Rogue?" Hydrocks said, blocking my way.

"Coffee. Need. Now." I replied.

Hydrocks looked upset. He seemed to have a chip on his shoulder or something. "If we want the upper hand on the orcs, we need to catch them by surprise," he claimed. "Coffee isn't going to win any battles today!"

I yawned in his face, before he marched over to Keeblur and started barking orders at him. Miss Fields just stood there yawning, pulling her hair into a ponytail. Voordman led us downstairs and distracted Hydrocks with some tactical nonsense, while I snuck in the kitchen and made a pot of coffee. I poured it into my travel container and grabbed a few cups for my group.

It was about 4:30 a.m. when we arrived at the scouting post and it was looking pretty quiet. Hydrocks gathered us around a tree, about ten yards from the front, and started going over different strategies. While he did that, I wandered over and leaned on the side of the front door and poured myself a cup of hot java. "Is that coffee I smell?' came a voice from the now cracked open door.

"Uh huh," I whispered, taking a long whiff from the cup in my hand.

"Do you have any idea what time it is?" yawned the orc, who slowly opened the door a bit more. "Got any more?"

"Sure," I said, filling up an extra cup I brought. "See the milksop in the big armor over there?"

"Yeah," the orc said, while taking his first sip.

"It was all his idea," I stated. "I wanted to wait for morning."

"No kidding," he shrugged. "What a fool."

Another orc appeared in the doorway, removing his sleeping cap. "What's going on?"

His buddy explained and the second orc just groaned. "I didn't sign up for this. Should I get the troops?"

"I'll take care of this," I replied, waving my hand. "Hey, guys. The orcs want to wait for morning. You okay with that?"

Hydrocks jumped up and grabbed his sword, but before he could run over, Keeblur stuck his foot out and tripped the overzealous paladin. The rest of the team tied him to a tree and we all agreed to a good fight in the morning.

I knew Hydrocks would be mad for a while, but all of his ideas were just half-baked anyway. I fell asleep on the cool night grass, as I heard him curse me through his mouth gag. "Oh well, he's young," I thought. He'll learn, soon enough, that's just how the cookie crumbles.

Entry 118

I was traveling through Miftenmad with my companions, Healy the Cleric and Fodderman the Zombie, when we received an urgent message from Logtoss the Dwarf that we should meet him in Horkenspit, in the Realm of Darkmist. The powerful fighter was capable of handling almost anything, so when we got his message, we knew it must involve something too big for him to handle.

It took a few days to get to the city, and when we did, we were shocked by the quietness. People were milling about the town and performing whatever daily tasks they needed. But, none of them were talking. Healy noticed how pale they were and we began to suspect vampires. Sometimes, they like to bite people and turn them into their daylight drones.

We dismissed that idea when people started noticing us and waving hello. They didn't seem to notice or acknowledge anyone else; only us. "These can't be drones," Healy whispered to me. "Drones wouldn't be nice; they'd just try to subdue us."

We made way for the Two Wolves Tavern, where Logtoss said to meet him. The owner, a ranger, named River Willow, showed us to the dwarf's table. Logtoss, like the others, was pale and had a huge smile on his face. "I'm so glad to see you," he commented. "You two look healthy!"

Healy and I knew something was up, because Logtoss never gave compliments. Honestly, he was a crusty, old codger, who would rather insult your mother or pass wind at a funeral, loudly. Healy and I approached him cautiously. "We came as fast as we could," Healy said. "Tell me you found us some work..."

Logtoss rubbed his beard and grinned. "Sure have. As a matter of fact, I want you to meet your new boss."

He motioned for us to turn around. When we did, we both stood almost face-to-face with an incredibly muscled, strong-jawed human fighter with bright blue eyes and shoulder length dark hair. He stuck out his hand for Healy and I saw the image of him just kind of flicker on and off. I shook my head, like something had gone loose, but there it was again. There was something about this man that didn't seem right.

I noticed that, while Healy was shaking his hand, he had gone stiff, like he just froze in place. At that moment, the man turned his head toward me and smiled. I felt ease like never before, like everything was going to be okay, but for some reason, because this was not my nature, I closed my human eye and only looked through my lich eye. Within moments, I shook the unnatural feelings off and saw this man for what he was: a hypnotick.

The tall, handsome man stood before me no longer; it was a two-foot-tall, black shelled, multi-legged tick with a stalk that protruded from the top of its head. There was an extra eye that gazed at me from the stalk, and it seemed to pulsate with energy.

That was it! This hideous little creature was hypnotizing the entire town and draining them of their blood. I'm surprised it hadn't run for mayor! When the creature thought I was hypnotized, it turned to Fodderman. It mustn't have known that he was an undead, because he was our traveling companion. It tried and tried to hypnotize him and was soon grabbing him in frustration, nearly jamming poor Fodderman in the eye with its gross eyestalk.

You'd think a unique creature like this would be hard to kill, but it wasn't. I removed my boot and started beating it into a pile of mushy goo. No better way to kill a bug, I guess. Within a few hours, the effects from the hypnotick wore off, and the people of the town were back to themselves. Mind you; they may have all been a few gold coins lighter!

Entry 119

I have to admit, once in a while, I too, am caught off guard by the strange things that happen in the Unremembered Realms. Like the time I was traveling through the Faerwood Forest down from the northern city of Dockport. They were beginning to celebrate one of the realms' endless festivals and I didn't want anything to do with the celebrations. Every year, it was the same old thing, and I was getting tired of the lame hallmonk holiday. In case you didn't know, hallmonks make cards at their temple and rake in money selling them to rubes for almost any occasion. I wish I would have thought of it first!

I was hoping to get to my girlfriend, Amberfawn's, place before nightfall, so I could enjoy a nice meal with her under the stars. But, as usual, something strange was going on in this magical forest and I couldn't resist the urge to investigate. I heard a horse whinnying and some loud and gruff laughter. I snuck my way through a clearing and saw a monstrous tree with a large, ugly barkskin face on its trunk and it was laughing. At first, I thought it was a Bothersome tree, but this one's branches were filled with the corpses of many travelers in various states of decay.

The branches would pick up the unsuspecting victim and use tendril like roots to drain its prey, until it was just a husk. I had heard of these trees before. They were known as Rootbeards, because of the extra drainage roots that grew around their mouths. I would have run at this point, but I recognized the brown horse with the white circle around its eye...Encumbrance!

I guess I owed the mare a favor, so I activated my blending cloak and ran up to the low hanging branch that had a grip on the horse and slashed at it with my dagger, Magurk. The tree let out a yelp, then grabbed at me, as Encumbrance fell to the ground. I dodged quickly and avoided its grasp. I started to run over to Encumbrance, as she stood up next to the trunk, and another branch caught hold of me. I managed to wiggle free, but the branch took my magical cloak off in the struggle.

As I jumped on Encumbrance, she back kicked the tree in the face and it let out a horrible yell. I rode the horse south for nearly ten minutes before I could calm her enough to slow down. When she did, I gave her a pat. I was just happy my friend was okay, but then starting to feel angry about the whole situation. That tree almost ate Encumbrance and snagged my cloak. I was determined to get it back.

As we rode toward Amberfawn's place, I came up with an idea. "Let's go visit Veedo the Wizard before we meet up with Amberfawn," I said to Encumbrance. "I think the both of them will be able to help in this situation."

The next day, Encumbrance, Amberfawn, Veedo, and I emerged from the woods into the clearing where the Rootbeard patiently waited for future victims. It still had a black ring around its eye where the horse had kicked it. "Your back," it's deep, crusty voice exclaimed, "and you've brought desert!"

The tree laughed so hard, a few skeletons fell from its upper branches and crashed to pieces on the ground. "I've come to claim what's mine," I explained, pointing to the cloak hanging from its branch.

"I've eaten thousands of souls before you were born," sneered the tree, its mouth roots writhing around. "What makes you think I care what you think, morsel!"

I held up a vial filled with black particles for the tree to see and stepped up a couple of feet. "I've got ways to convince you to return it."

The tree laughed even harder now. "Poison?! Fool! Your silly poisons won't work on me. I am poison!"

Amberfawn quickly grabbed the vial from my hand, as I popped the cork and she flew through the branches of the tree, emptying it as she flew. The tree was so unconcerned, that it didn't pay attention to the tiny faerie. It only kept its eyes on me. "Come now, come take your cloak."

"I will, in a minute," I replied, as I walked over to Encumbrance and stroked her mane. "We have to give the termites a little time. They are a little slow, being pregnant and all."

"What?!" the tree yelled, before sneezing loudly. "What did you say?!"

"Termoots!" Veedo said, stepping forward. "Magigull termoots! Verily deadly to trees!"

"Aaahh!!!" the tree screamed and sneezed again. "Get them off me! Get them off me! I'll do anything!"

I walked over to the tree, and it lowered its branch to give me my cloak back; which, I slipped on quickly. "Now for the rest..." I told him.

Reluctantly, the tree lowered all the corpses down to the ground and Veedo and I inspected them for goodies. Veedo found a spell book and a magical staff, while I got nearly my own weight in coins. The tree whimpered in agony, as it watched us load up Encumbrance. "Help me!" begged the tree. "You have to get rid of these!"

"You held up your part of the deal, so I'll hold up mine," I said, as I pulled a vial of white granules from my pocket. "It's a special blend of poison. It'll kill all the eggs."

"Thank you, thank you," the Rootbeard cried.

"But wait," I held up a finger. "Veedo made something magical for you."

Veedo opened up a pack on Encumbrance and brought out a handful of little bells tied to strings. "Theese arb libble collars," he garbled. "They keeb der bugs away. We poort out a bunch of their eggs indo the area, just in case."

The big tree frowned, but lowered its branches, again, so we could tie the bug resistant collars to it. Then, Amberfawn flew all over the tree, gently dropping the white granules over its branches and main trunk. "Ahh," the tree sighed. "I feel much better. But what's with the bells?"

"So others know you're here and don't end up as lunch," I explained. "The next time we're around, give us a ring!"

Amberfawn and Veedo laughed, as the big tree fumbled some response, while we walked off with Encumbrance back into the forest. After a while, we stopped for a bite. Amberfawn laughed when Veedo had pulled out more black and white vials, then sprinkled his food with them. "That was so sneaky," she said, while sitting on my shoulder. "I can't believe that old tree fell for it!"

"Good old salt and pepper," I chuckled. "They might not be magic, but they got to the root of our problem!

Entry 120

Rarely in one's travels, do you get to meet one of the real mysteries of the adventuring trade, the Master of the Dungeon. These are the people who work behind the scenes to keep quests alive in the Unremembered Realms. Do you think dungeons just happen to build themselves? Have you taken time to consider the unlikely collaboration between various monsters, who shouldn't be able to get along?

I had only heard about Masters of Dungeons, or MD for short, but one time I had the distinct pleasure of bumping into one. I was in the deepest layer of the Morkenhoin Dungeon, in Darkmist, with my party of fellow adventurers, when I stumbled through an illusionary doorway. It appeared to be a solid stone wall, but I passed, effortlessly, through it. Sitting at a table with another fellow arguing over some handbook, was a real life Master of the Dungeon.

Across the table, was a map of each layer of this dungeon, some drawing utensils, and dice. There were little figures dispersed throughout the map showing differing types of monsters in various locations, and even secret doors revealed on the map. "Who are you and what are you doing here?" demanded the MD.

I just smiled and started walking up to the table. That's when an ugly goblin came out of nowhere and tackled me to the floor. The creature pulled out a dagger, but didn't realize that mine was already at his throat. "Back off, Webster," the other mysterious figure told the goblin. "Let him up. I'm impressed with his skills."

"You're lucky, Webster," I said, standing up. "You wouldn't have

194

been the first goblin I've killed. Most wind up in a dumpster!"

Webster hissed at me, then backed himself into a poorly lit area of the room. "My name is ...."

"Don't bother telling us your name, rogue. We don't care..." the Master of the Dungeon said, not even looking up from his pile of notes. "What's important is you get back with your party and finish your quest. I need to see how this plays out, before everyone goes home tonight!"

"It may be an all-nighter," I told him, "but before I go, do you mind if I take a little peak at the dangers ahead?"

"Yeah, right!" the darker haired person next to him laughed. "That is not in the rules!"

The other person was what was known as a Rules Lawyer; someone who always pestered the Master of the Dungeon with handbooks and guides to keep the dungeon running smoothly. "Rules are made to be broken!" the MD snarled back. "Otherwise, nobody would have any fun!"

The Rules Lawyer did not like that. "Show me in the book where dungeon planning is supposed to be fun," he said, while waving a thick tome at the MD. "Go ahead, show me!"

I listened to them argue for about ten minutes, before I realized they weren't paying any attention at all to my presence. I quietly took out a scrap piece of a scroll and started making a copy of the layout that was on the table. Not long after that, the Rules Lawyer knocked over a bowl of snacks onto the map, toppling some the figures. "Look what you've done now, fool!" cried the Master of the Dungeon.

"Let me show you on page 36, it's in black and white, right here by the crummy cartoon!" the Rules Lawyer kept on. "Grab that twenty-sided dice over there. We'll go by this chart..."

I stepped back, pocketed my scroll, and tiptoed back toward the secret door. I stuck my tongue out at Webster, who sat quietly picking his nose as I passed him. Before I left, the last thing I heard was the Master of the Dungeon complaining, "Who drank the Morning Dew? That was my last one!"

When I caught up with my team, they were stunned that I was still alive. They were even more amazed and happy that I had a copy of the rest of the dungeon, with all the monsters listed and their locations. I never told them about what happened. I wasn't sure I understood it myself, but hey, I'm not one to complain about a happy ending.

IF YOU WOULD LIKE TO SEE MORE
ADVENTURES FROM THE OUTLAW,
PLEASE TAKE A MOMENT AND REVIEW
THIS BOOK ON YOUR FAVORITE BOOKSITE
LIKE AMAZON.COM. PLEASE SHARE ON
YOUR FAVORITE SOCIAL MEDIA AS WELL.

ABOUT THE AUTHOR

Mick McArt is the author of the "Journal of an Outlaw" comedy fantasy book. This is the first in a series taking place in the Unremembered Realms. Mick is also an illustrator and author of children's books, his most popular being the "Tales of Wordishure" series.

After a few television appearances he was asked to create a small Saturday morning art show on a local television station, TCT. He appears at book signings, art shows, comic cons, and also gives lectures at churches, schools, and colleges on independent publishing.

Mick is a full-time Multimedia Design that is currently running his own publishing company, Mick Art Productions Publishing, where he can help struggling independent authors get their books to market.

Currently, Mick is working on a Homeschool Art Curriculum for all ages. Micks family include his wife Erica, and their children Micah, Jonah, and Emerald. They currently live in Midland, Michigan.

Mick earned a Bachelor of Fine Arts degree from Central Michigan University in 1997 and a Masters degree from Saginaw Valley State University in 2006.

Made in the USA
Columbia, SC
11 March 2021